TIM MARKS

Foreword by New York Times, Wall Street Journal, and USA Today Best-Selling Author
ORRIN WOODWARD

VOYAGE OF A
VIKING

HOW A MAN OF ACTION
CAN BECOME A MAN OF GRACE

VOYAGE OF A VIKING

HOW A MAN OF ACTION
CAN BECOME A MAN OF GRACE

TIM MARKS

First Edition, April 2012

Published by:
Obstaclés Press Inc.
4072 Market Place Dr.
Flint, MI 48507

Cover design and layout by Norm Williams

Printed in the United States of America

To Amy

TABLE OF CONTENTS

FOREWORD

In today's age, many people blame others for their nonproductive lives, proclaiming themselves victims of society's mistreatment. Tim Marks's early life had all the signs that would qualify him for victimhood, with one extremely important difference: He refused to go along with society's labels. Tim's near-legendary success today— he has tens of thousands of people within his leadership community; is a keynote speaker in front of tens of thousands of people; and is a loving husband to his beautiful wife Amy and the father of four wonderful children—can easily overshadow his humble beginnings, which is why Tim's new book *Voyage of a Viking* is part autobiography, part personal development, and part leadership, all married into one.

When he shared his life story with me, I found myself pulling for young Tim as I listened to accounts of some of his early struggles with his education, his parents' divorce, and his latch-key childhood. Tim's stories of his dreams, struggles, and victories will inspire millions of others who started out on the "wrong side of the tracks." It's so easy to see the finished product without realizing the arduous journey taken in order to achieve it. Few people have overcome as many obstacles in so short a time as Tim has. So many lessons are taught through his stories that I found myself in awe of his overcoming spirit and God's redeeming grace.

In this book, Tim will share the key principles of personal development that helped him on his journey from being a Viking to achieving victory. I have had the honor of mentoring hundreds of leaders over the last eighteen years, and I have been working with Tim for the last twelve years. Not one of those I personally mentored moved from problem identified to problem solved as quickly as

Tim Marks did! In fact, Tim's ability to confront issues and change is directly related to his humility. Instead of defending his ego and sacrificing excellence, Tim chooses to defend excellence by sacrificing his ego. The lessons he teaches as he recounts his Viking journey will enhance the life of everyone who reads this book.

Tim captures the essence of leadership by example. Tim lives the thirteen principles that I share in my book *RESOLVED: 13 Resolutions for LIFE*.[1] Remember, example is not the main thing in leadership — it's the only thing. Tim leads by example in everything that he does, whether it's by encouraging the downhearted, loving the unlovable, courageously confronting defeats, or celebrating the victory of others. Tim started out as a student of leadership and then graduated as one of the best teachers and examples of leadership in America today. Moreover, I find that I learn just as much from Tim as I teach because he has become a man of grace — not to mention that he has become one of my best friends and a person whom I trust unconditionally.

Tim and Amy Marks's story should be shared around the world. At a time when heroes are nearly an extinct species, their story is a reminder that with courage and the right principles, heroic lives are still possible. Don't just read this book; devour it! Choose to live and lead with the principles in this book, becoming another example of what God's grace can do in a person's life. What are you waiting for? Isn't it time you start your learning voyage through the Viking's life and leadership?

Orrin Woodward
Founder of LIFE
Top 10 (IAB) Independent Association of Business Leader
Port St. Lucie, Florida

ACKNOWLEDGMENTS

One thing I have learned in the process of writing this book is that completing it required not just the months involved in putting it together but, even more, the lifelong struggle, the learning process, and the many people who loved me and taught me things along the way.

I want to thank all the people who helped make this book possible. First, I offer my gratitude to Sarah Ascol for her many hours of research and editing. Thanks to my writer, CJ Calvert, for his dedication and commitment to getting this project done and (We hope!) done right. Thanks to best-selling author and my great friend Chris Brady. Without his encouragement in my office one afternoon, this book would not have happened. Chris and his wife Terri have been such great mentors to Amy and me through the years.

I also want to thank my pastor Dr. Tom Ascol of Grace Baptist Church in Cape Coral, Florida, for teaching me the biblical truths and, most importantly, for living the truths that he teaches. It has been, and continues to be, a blessing to sit under his ministry.

My sincere appreciation goes to the most influential man in my life — my mentor, the best-selling author Orrin Woodward — and to his wife Laurie for being such amazing friends to my wife Amy and me and teaching us so much about business and life.

Although my mom Sandy Marks passed away in 1996, she is still an influence in my life through all the lessons she taught me while I was growing up. She was my hero, and I miss her greatly.

In addition, I want to thank all of my children — Cameron, Mya, Nash, and Max — for sticking with Daddy and giving me grace while I took the time I required to work on this project. More importantly, you are all a big part of the reason I wrote this book. So, kids, please learn from my lessons and know Daddy loves you and is committed to putting in his full effort to do the best he can for you.

How can I put into words my gratitude for the most important person on earth to me, my beautiful wife Amy? She has been, and always will be, the best person to encourage me when I'm down, and she has always filled in the gaps. (With me, that's a high calling.) Her wisdom and insight, particularly in dealing with people, have been priceless to me in learning and growing as a father and a business leader. As I type these words, we are approaching twenty years of marriage and, God willing, many more to come. I love you, Amy Marks.

Finally, I want to thank my Lord and Savior Jesus Christ and praise Him for all the grace and blessings in our lives.

INTRODUCTION

Make it your business to know yourself, which is the most difficult lesson in the world.[2]

—Miguel De Cervantes

In the movie *Gods and Generals*, a young soldier walks with General Andrew "Stonewall" Jackson as they survey the aftermath of battle. Bodies lie lifeless on the field around them, and Jackson reaches out with a gloved hand to close the eyes of one man who has fallen. The young soldier beside him, overwhelmed by the carnage, asks, "General, how is it you can keep so serene and stay so utterly insensible, with a storm of shells and bullets raining about your head?"[3]

Without hesitation, Jackson replies, "My religious belief teaches me to feel as safe in battle as in bed. God has fixed the time for my death. I do not concern myself with that. But to be always ready, whenever it may overtake me—*that* is the way all men should live. Then all men would be equally brave."[4]

I love that quote because it's what I really believe, and it's how I try to live each day. The place that I choose to draw my strength from is my Lord. I shake my head and wonder where other people choose to draw their strength. When I compare the amount of bravery of modern-day Americans with the heroism of the fighting men of World War II, it saddens me to admit that we don't see enough examples of courage in our daily lives today.

I have always had respect for a certain type of courage. If you would have asked the old Tim, I would have given you one very narrow definition of bravery— that of men in battle. I would have first thought of bravery as being something that our young soldiers have when they serve overseas, risking their lives to defend the freedom of people around the world. I also have a lot of respect for a firefighter who runs into a burning building to save a child, or a police officer who breaks up a domestic dispute.

But bravery doesn't have to involve physical risk. You might see bravery in a whistleblower standing up to the leaders of a company with unethical practices, or in an employee risking his job because he won't fudge the numbers at tax time. Bravery can be seen when a man chooses to become the husband and father that he should be, instead of walking out of the house or getting a divorce. Bravery can be seen in our kids when they stand up for a classmate who is being bullied, or when they risk being laughed at for not accepting a beer at a party. Bravery can be seen when you have a courageous conversation with a friend, and it can be seen when you have the guts to start a business of your own.

While I've always tried to be a guy who is quick to stand up for what I believe in, my "Ready, *fire*, aim" style has sometimes hurt people in the process. My mistake had been that I used to think that all you need to win are guts and determination. Sure, those are important ingredients for success—critical, even. But it took me a lot of time, and a lot of prayer, to realize that the missing ingredient in my journey wasn't *courage*—it was *compassion*.

> It took me a lot of time, and a lot of prayer, to realize that the missing ingredient for me in my journey wasn't courage— it was compassion.

"Courage without compassion" describes exactly the type of guy I used to be. It's like being a bull running through a china shop; you sure reach your destination, but you leave a heck of a mess behind you. I won every battle I fought and didn't stop to notice whom I stepped on during the fight. In fact, I actually found it funny that no one ever stood up to me. Really, no one dared.

I had such a harsh exterior, with so many rough edges in my personality, that I eventually earned a nickname at work. It wasn't a nickname that you'd bestow on a cute little baby or on a boss you looked up to. Nope, this was a nickname that carried some negativity with it. I was a fighter, but not one you'd want to spend any time hanging out with after the smoke cleared. I wasn't a Compassionate Samurai,[5] or even a Jedi Knight.[6] I was known as the Viking. And that nickname wasn't a compliment.

As time went on, I realized I needed to change. I had to stop being the Viking. But change can be scary, especially when it means changing how we act and think. And that's when I learned that there is yet another type of bravery. It's a courage that doesn't involve confronting other people—it involves confronting the man in the mirror. One of the highest forms of bravery we can show is doing the tough work of *changing ourselves*.

> *One of the highest forms of bravery we can show is doing the tough work of* changing ourselves.

My goal for this book is to make the readers feel, as they read the stories of my mistakes and the lessons I've learned along the way, that if I can change, they can change. This is a book about shaking off our bad habits and bad attitudes and revealing the champion inside each of us. It's a story of letting go of anger and sadness and forgiving ourselves for our sinful ways. It's a story of casting off the hard shell around our hearts and becoming everything God meant us to be.

This is the story of a guy who decided that winning the war of success wasn't worth the price if it meant stepping on the toes of his family and friends. I had to change from being a man of action into a man of grace. I hope that in telling my story, I don't come across as self-promoting. The Lord knows, as does everyone around me, both how far I have come and how far I have yet to go. I'm still learning every day, and I plan to keep on learning. But I trust that if you're facing some of the same struggles that I have faced, you may see yourself in my story, and it may give you hope.

Become the Best Version of Yourself

When I was a child, I spoke like a child, I thought like a child, I reasoned like a child. When I became a man, I gave up childish ways. For now we see in a mirror dimly, but then face to face. Now I know in part; then I shall know fully, even as I have been fully known.

—1 Corinthians 13:11–12 (English Standard Version)

One of the problems that riddle society today is that, especially with the Internet, there is a lot of information available but not a lot of wisdom. It would be tough for almost anybody to sort through all of the noise and figure out to whom one should listen. Because of this, I felt it was time to share some of the lessons I've learned so far along my journey in the hopes that they would be a greater blessing to you.

I don't expect you to imitate me or to go after the exact same goals that I have. I want you to become *you* – the *best* version of you. I love what Og Mandino says: "There is only one of you, so you are rare. There is value in rarity. Therefore, you are valuable."[7] No one else can ever be you, and here's your chance to turn over a new leaf and become the best you. If you think you can become more courageous, let's work on that. If you think you can become more loving to your family, I hope this book inspires you to do so. And if you have some rough edges in your personality, there is hope for change. Believe me, I've had to do a lot of work in that department myself.

I'm certainly not an expert, but perhaps I'm a little farther down the path in some areas than you may be; I wouldn't be surprised if there are many things that you are better at than I am. I'm not a genius by any stretch of the imagination, but at least I'm smart enough to know that I'm dumb about some stuff. It keeps me hungry to learn and grow and to achieve all that God meant for me.

Throughout this book, I'm going to share some deeply personal stories—warts and all. I'll reveal secrets that have never been shared from the stage or the podium, things that shook me to the core and that even my family members will just now be learning through the launch of this book. As you make your way through this book, we will discuss the following:

- **Chapter 1: Am I a Victim or a Viking?**
  We've each probably faced some childhood disappointments and made some youthful mistakes. I will share some of mine. I will also tell you about how I struggled to not allow those hurtful moments to define me. We will discuss how each of us has a choice to become bitter or better.

- **Chapter 2: From Viking to Superman**
  I'll discuss how bad things had gotten in my marriage, my calculated gamble with real estate, and my desperate race to go from financial disaster to "making it." I promise that the stories won't glorify me; they will show the good, the bad, and the ugly. I believe that if I share my mistakes, someone can learn from them and avoid the same pain that I caused myself. If you find yourself having fallen down in your responsibilities as a spouse or a parent and feel your heart drifting away, I suggest you read, in particular, the story of how I came to turn things around in my marriage and in my relationship with my kids.

- **Chapter 3: The Character of a Viking**
  If you've ever wondered how to toughen up, or how to soften up, we'll discuss both the strengths and weaknesses of being a Viking. I'll offer a bunch of ideas from which you can choose the ones that will work best for you. Since everyone has a different personality, I recommend you eat the meat and spit out the bones. We'll discuss how my faith helped me begin to rub out my rough edges and love people where they are. We'll talk about what it means to take action, go after what you want, and be a blessing to people in the process.

- **Chapter 4: Live on Results Food**
  In this chapter, I'm going to challenge you to be productive, not just busy. This is a no-holds-barred discussion on the speed of the leader determining the speed of the group. You have to face your reality if you want to win, and being honest with yourself and evaluating your true performance can be a little scary. But in order to create massive change, you have to set massive goals. Playing small gets you small rewards. You have more talent and ability inside you than you realize, and I hope to remove some of the doubts and push you out of your comfort zone to become the best you can be. As William Carey said, "We have only to keep the end in view and have our hearts thoroughly engaged in the pursuit of it, and the means will not be very difficult."[8]

- **Chapter 5: All Warriors Have Wounds to Be Mended**
  In the battle to create your greatest life possible, it's fair to expect that you're going to get knocked down. Champions get back up. But there is a time for rest and healing, and we need to be graceful with ourselves and others when we are struggling to find our footing on the battlefield. Endurance, perseverance, and the ability to soldier on despite crushing setbacks are what separate the men from the boys.

- **Chapter 6: Work Hard, Play Hard, and Live with Purpose**
  Champions need to know when to sprint and when to celebrate. If you go after every goal with grim determination, you may find the road longer and harder than it needs to be. Remember, even God took a day off. (But not for Him—for us!) Learning to develop a spirit of fun, camaraderie, and joy in the journey is an often-forgotten principle. My business partners and I have long said, "Have fun, make money, and make a difference," and we put "Have fun" at the top of the list for a reason.

I want to congratulate you for taking the time to read this book, and I hope that it will be instrumental in your endeavor to learn and grow. It takes a special type of person to turn off the television and seek wisdom. Just by the very fact that you have a hunger to learn, I know that you are a special person. I hope that the insights in these pages will truly help you to live intentionally for excellence.

Let's get cranking!

Am I a Victim or a Viking?

Successful people start out in life with the same disadvantages as the rest of us. They just find ways to turn their disadvantages into assets. [9]

—Sidney A. Friedman

As the saying goes, "We don't get to choose the hand we're dealt; we only get to choose how we play the cards." We all start where we start, good or bad. Some people have the advantage of loving parents, a stable family, a good neighborhood, and money coming into the house. Some people start on the wrong side of the tracks and fight their way to the top.

> *Some people have sight, but no vision for success.*

Some people have sight, but no vision for success. And some people are born blind, but they have a great vision for how they can inspire people.

We each have our victories and our sorrows. I have had my tough times, and I'm sure you have had yours as well. As I share some of my story, the last thing I want you to think is, "Oh, poor Tim." It is my hope that—whatever circumstances you have faced, or are currently facing—you feel that if I, Tim Marks, could make it through, so can you. The most important point of my story is to give perspective, which is why I love to study other people, so that we can learn to overcome the baggage from the past and work on becoming better people. If something is holding us back from getting the life we want, maybe it's time to let go of our baggage.

My story is probably similar in many ways to your story. Everyone I've ever met has had some defining moments that shaped his or her life, and I'm no different. Maybe your defining moment as a kid was when your dad first threw a softball to you in the backyard, and you discovered that you were pretty good at playing catch. Maybe your parents took you swimming at the lake near your cottage one summer, and you slipped and fell in the water and developed a fear of water. Maybe your dad took you to the movies one Saturday afternoon to see your favorite superhero save the day, and you decided that one day you would be a hero and save people, too. Or maybe, just like me, your first defining moment was the day your mom and your dad got divorced, and your world was turned upside down.

YOU DON'T HAVE A DAD, TIM

I cannot think of any need in childhood as strong as the need for a father's protection.[10]

—Sigmund Freud

This is probably as good a place to start as any, since it had such a big effect on me in so many ways, all the way into my adulthood. When you're a kid though, things that are pretty big don't always seem that big at the time. It didn't seem like a big deal that Saturday afternoon when my parents announced that they were getting a divorce. My brother John and I were horsing around upstairs when we heard my mom call us down. She and Dad were sitting on the couch looking pretty grim. Then they dropped the bomb on us: They were splitting up.

I remember that at the moment, it didn't really register with me what they were talking about. I just shrugged and said, "Okay," and went back to playing. It didn't sink in that our family just got smashed into little pieces. It didn't sink in that Dad wasn't going to be around anymore. It kind of felt as though Dad was just announcing that he was going out for a while and would be back by supper. Maybe my little six-year-old brain didn't understand it, or maybe I didn't want to hear it. But I soon realized that it would have a pretty big impact on me.

Schoolyard Trouble

Undeservedly you will atone for the sins of your fathers.[11]

—Horace

The reality of the divorce started sinking in. My folks didn't have a fifty-fifty arrangement; I didn't even see my dad every second weekend, as is the arrangement in many divorces today. Instead, I would see him once every six weeks, and then only for a few hours. It seemed as though he had disappeared. My heartache began in earnest by this time.

I would ride my bike home two miles from school, even at six years old, and find the house empty – no Mom, no Dad. My brother was nine at the time; sometimes he was there, and sometimes he was out playing. We both dealt with the divorce in our own ways. I would get home, and all the lights would be off, and the house would feel very empty. I was only six, and I was alone for several hours each day before my mom would be home from work. We hardly ever had a babysitter. Sometimes Mom was able to arrange for the neighbor's girl to check in on us. You have to remember that this was the late '70s, and divorce just wasn't as prevalent as it is today. My mom was pretty much the only divorced mom in the whole neighborhood, so our family stuck out like a sore thumb.

Kids can be pretty relentless in teasing one another, and the kids in my school were no different. I had never before been the subject of teasing and bullying, so it was a new experience for me. You see, news of my parents' divorce got around town pretty quickly, and it wasn't too long before the news hit my schoolyard. And then the teasing began.

"There's Tim, and he doesn't have a dad," the kids would whisper to each other and taunt me. Back then, like today, I was a "less talk, more action" kind of guy. The kids' teasing started to get under my skin, so I reacted in a very diplomatic way: I pounded the snot out of them. While my little six-year-old mouth didn't have the words to respond, my fists sure did. It's amazing how much of a wallop those little fists of mine had; my anger and hurt added a little oomph to each punch. It took only a few beatings before the kids decided to back off.

One time, even my cousin laid into me, teasing me about my dad leaving. I just exploded in rage, and I pounded him, too. My uncle had to haul me off of him, but not before I had landed a few good hits. It was a good six months before I spoke to my cousin again. (We ended up being drinking buddies later on, but back then, I was pretty angry at him.) My uncle was very upset with me; he pulled me off of my cousin and threw me, yelling, "Get the hell out of here!" I felt as if I'd been kicked in the gut. When he yelled at me like that, I saw it as even more rejection from another father figure. My little boy's heart felt as though it had been broken into a hundred pieces.

Coming out of school each day was a tough thing. I would unlock my bike from the bike rack and watch the other moms or dads pick up their kids. I would watch them get out of their cars in their work suits and pat their kids on the head, and I wondered how great it would be if my dad would pick me up. I wondered if those kids' dads would take them out to dinner, or if their dads would take them to the park to throw a ball around. I would stare at them while feeling empty inside, wondering, "Why don't I have a dad?" Then I went home to be alone.

This was all starting to get to me. I didn't understand why, but I started wanting to go to the nurse's office all the time. I was aching inside. I would complain that I was feeling sick and that I couldn't be in class; I just wanted to curl up into a ball on the cot in the sickroom. My mom would be at work; she couldn't get me, so the nurse would call my uncle or my grandparents. The nurse would take my temperature, and the thermometer would indicate that my temperature was normal.

My grandparents or my uncle would pick me up, and when they would discover I didn't have a fever, they would scold me for malingering. They would yell at me, "You aren't sick! There is nothing wrong with you!" But I knew I wasn't fine, and I knew I wasn't fibbing. I just felt awful. I would start crying and wonder, "Why can't my dad come home?" I just wanted to get out of school because of the pain, but going home didn't get rid of the pain either. I just didn't know what to do; I was just a confused kid.

The Canoe Trip

The words that a father speaks to his children in the privacy of home are not heard by the world, but, as in whispering galleries, they are clearly heard at the end, and by posterity.[12]
—Jean Paul Richter

It's amazing, the little moments from childhood, both good and bad, that get burned into your memory forever. One of my worst memories of feeling abandoned by my dad was when I was in sixth grade. My mom had gotten me involved in the Cub Scouts, and I found that I really enjoyed it. It was something to do, and I got along pretty well with the other kids. I thought it was a great program, and I still believe in it today. It molds character and teaches leadership skills, teamwork, and responsibility. It provided me a group of buddies to hang around with and seemed like a good way to keep me out of trouble.

The Cub Scouts were going on a weekend father-and-son canoe trip on some river in Northern Michigan. As you can imagine, there was one pretty clear criterion to meet for this father-and-son canoe trip: Each kid needed his dad to go with him. At all the Cub Scout meetings that month, the guys kept talking about how much fun the canoe trip was going to be: canoeing and portaging like wilderness explorers, hiking and camping, building fires, and cooking s'mores. It sure sounded like a blast. I couldn't wait to tell my dad about it. I knew for sure that he would come.

I told all the other kids, "My dad is going to be there, and we'll race you in the canoes!" It was the sort of talk that little kids flung around, the sort of verbal sparring that says, "My dad is stronger than your dad." And the kids laughed and said, "Yeah, right. Your dad lives in Ohio, and you live in Michigan. He's never around. He's not coming." I told myself that my dad was coming because I wanted so badly for what I said to be true.

I remember my mom being suspicious as to whether or not my dad would show up. She probably figured he wasn't coming but didn't have the heart to tell me.

The morning of the trip, my mom brought me to the mall to meet Dad. She asked if I wouldn't rather wait for him at home. I assured her that Dad would be picking me up and that I would be fine. After all, I was certain he would come. I had the directions to the lake all written down. I had packed my clothes, brought my sleeping bag, and was wearing my camping outfit. I was very excited. I thought it was going to be a great adventure.

I remember sitting in the car with Mom for a while outside the mall. Soon I stopped looking at my watch. I finally realized that my dad wasn't coming. I had wanted so much to believe that he would be there, but I finally faced the fact that the canoe trip was not going to happen for me. I don't remember all the details, but I remember that my mom was upset. She was cussing, and we eventually drove back home.

Even now, I still don't have an idea what happened that day. I remember that I started thinking about my dad, and not in a positive way. I started thinking about how he had left us and was hardly around for John and me. I started thinking about how bad I felt since he walked out and how angry I was at him for what he did.

That very day, I made a life-changing decision that will last till the day I die. I decided that when I grew up, I would be a *great* dad. I would be the *best* dad I could be. The hurt of that moment was so deep that I set a goal right there that when I had kids, I would *never* do anything to make them feel the way I felt right then. I never wanted my future kids to live with the same bad feelings and to go through the same painful experiences I did while growing up. As it turned out, not having a father has been the best thing that has ever happened for my relationship with my kids

In fact, that lesson rings true today with my four kids. I had resolved that I would be there for my kids. I would put aside my free time and sacrifice for my kids. For example, one week, I sat out for three hours in the 96-degree

> *Not having a father has been the best thing that has ever happened for my relationship with my kids.*

Florida weather to be at my boy's first football practice because it was important to him. He wanted me to be on the sidelines for his first practice. I looked around, and there was just me and one other guy out there; all the other parents were sitting in air-conditioned cars. I am willing to do stuff like that because I love my kids, and I never ever want them to go through my pain — the pain of not having a dad around to offer me support and encouragement.

I have learned that God hates divorce; it's very tough on the kids. It's hard on the parents, but it's really harder on the kids. I've shared this story with you because there might be a dad, or even a mom, who is thinking of walking out of the house and away

> *God hates divorce; it's very tough on the kids.*

from his or her marriage. If you are struggling in your marriage, you have my empathy. I don't know your story, and it's not my place to judge your circumstances. But I want you to consider that if you do walk away from a troubled marriage, maybe you are leaving your kids behind, too.

Orrin Woodward says, "You can't fix a marriage if you leave." Sometimes we need to choose to stay in the house for the kids' sake, out of duty to them, even when the affection has faded in the marriage. Do it out of commitment to your kids, not to mention for the commitment you

> You can't fix a marriage
> if you leave.
> – Orrin Woodward

made when you stated your marriage vows before God. Reach out for help from your pastor, a mentor, a friend, or a counselor. Reach out for help by falling to your knees and reaching up. Try just a little while longer; it might make all the difference to your kids, as it would have made a difference to me.

YOU'RE DUMB, TIM

No man is defeated without until he has first been defeated within.[13]

—Eleanor Roosevelt

Some people discover pretty early on what their talents are; they might be great at soccer or math, or they might be popular with other kids. For other people, including me, it takes a little while longer to figure some of this stuff out. It wasn't clear to me in the beginning what I was good at. What was very, very clear, however, especially to me, was that I was *not* good at school.

I had managed to get along pretty well academically in kindergarten and the first grade because it wasn't very mentally demanding. But by the second grade, the heat was on, and I was toast. My first memories of my academic troubles were definitely in the second grade. Whether it was being called to the front of the room to do math problems or to read out loud from a book, I just couldn't measure up against anyone else in my class.

If the teacher called me up to the front of the class, I would stand and stare at the board, chalk in hand, and just freeze in terror. I could feel the embarrassment building up and hear all the whispering of the kids behind me. Every second I stood at that board, I grew more and more nervous, until I couldn't take it anymore. The problem really wasn't that I was bad at math; the real problem was that my confidence was in the toilet. I would freeze, and I couldn't figure it out. The more I froze, the more I couldn't think; it was a vicious cycle. I would walk back to my chair, and I couldn't look anyone in the eye.

I felt so terrified of standing up in front of that board and embarrassing myself again that if I thought the teacher was going to call on me, I would literally excuse myself to go to the bathroom. (We had one in our classroom.) And I would hide in there until I heard her call on someone else. These moments would birth in me, much like what happens with many other people, a fear of speaking in front of groups. The embarrassment felt suffocating.

Reading was even worse. Even if it was a simple book, whenever I got called upon to read, I would turn beet red and feel nauseated; sometimes I actually thought I was going to be sick. I was just too embarrassed to read because I read very slowly. I knew it seemed strange to the other kids that it took me a long time to read, but it was so difficult for me. When I read to myself, I would read it, and a moment later, I couldn't remember what I had read. I couldn't understand why the words looked as if they moved around on the page. I would struggle with the same word over and over. But as a little kid, neither I nor my mom or my teachers knew that I was dyslexic, let alone that I had a case of ADD.

This ignorance of my condition made everyone, including me, think that I was simply either lazy or stupid. Of course, my nerves made it worse. I was extremely nervous any time I had to read out loud. I could not pronounce the words. It seemed to me that everyone was smarter than I was. Normally, if you were not feeling too smart, there was always at least one kid who was the class nimrod that you could point to and say, "At least I'm smarter than that guy!" But I didn't even have that. I *was* the nimrod, and everyone pointed at me.

In fact, a booger-eating kid named Dan and I were what made the upper 95 percent of the class possible!

Today, three decades later, when I preach or speak at a leadership conference, I have to read from notes, and I still need to practice several times in advance to make sure that I understand the words so that they don't jump around on the page. My reading still isn't where it should be, but it's a heck of a lot better than it was!

Negative Association Forms Negative Habits

If you want to be a winner, hang around with winners.[14]
—Christopher D. Furman

The power of association must not be underestimated. Whatever you put into your brain is going to stick. Whatever you watch, read, or listen to is going to change the way you think. Whoever you hang around with is going to change the way you think. And because of that, we as adults have to be very careful to monitor what goes into our heads. But as little kids, we just have to hope that Mom and Dad have learned this lesson already for our benefit.

> *The power of association must not be underestimated.*

When I was in the third grade, my class had a monthly film showing. My teacher would go to the library and pick out a movie, and we'd have a blast. (It was a great way of taking a break from our academic work.) One month, the movie was about lumberjacks. I remember watching the movie and seeing this big, tough lumberjack biting a big chunk of chewing tobacco and chewing away at it.

For some reason, that image really stuck in my brain. I was really curious what the big deal was with chewing tobacco, and I wanted to find out. That very night, after school, I took some money from my piggy bank, and I walked to the local gas station to buy some chewing tobacco. And the really terrible part of the story is that they sold it to me without hesitation. Can you imagine them selling this stuff to a third grader? Maybe they figured I was buying it for my dad.

I remember the label said, "Levi Garrett Chewing Tobacco." I couldn't wait to get it unwrapped. I ripped off the packaging, scooped it up, and took a big bite. I started chewing. After only a few moments, I thought to myself, "Man, this stuff doesn't taste very good!" Well, I was used to chewing gum, and whenever I had chewing gum in class that I needed to get rid of, I just swallowed it. So just to get it over with, I swallowed the big hunk of chewing tobacco! No one told me you're not supposed to do that!

A few minutes later, I was walking home and crossing over a bridge. Well, the chewing tobacco was working its magic on my guts, and all of a sudden, I grabbed the railing and just started heaving over the side. I tossed the package over the side of the bridge, and that was the first and last time I ever tried Levi Garrett. Why did I share this story? I shared it because of what it illustrates about association: I saw something in a movie, and it got inside my head and started whispering to me to do something silly that day. And this was just from watching one movie. The media programs our brain every day, and the brains of our little kids. We have to always be very careful with what we expose our families to. Whether it's *Little House on the Prairie* on one end or Cheech and Chong on the other, that's the power of programming. As I got older, negative association also introduced me to other unhealthy habits. Growing up, I was exposed to a lot of smoking. My mom had a lot of friends over, and they would all smoke and drink along with her. My mom only smoked when she was drinking, but I looked at her friends and thought they were cool. That's an easy-enough sell to a young kid: If you want to look cool, smoke like the "cool" people do. Advertisers have been singing that song for years. Then whenever I was around my dad, he would smoke as well. And like many young guys, I wanted to copy what my dad did. Since he smoked, I decided that I wanted to smoke, too.

I'll hear smokers explain that they are going to tell their kids not to smoke. If you think this way, I hate to break it to you, but if you smoke, your kids are probably going to want to imitate you! We can't lead our households by announcing to our kids, "Do as I say and not as I do." Our kids know that that does not hold any weight, and we should, too.

> *We cannot lead our households by announcing to our kids, "Do as I say and not as I do." Our kids know that that does not hold any weight, and we should, too.*

The first time I really remember smoking was in sixth grade. One of the kids who lived in a house behind us was always smoking. He was probably in ninth grade at the time. We ended up outside together when he was heading out to smoke. He simply handed me one and said, "Here you go!" I didn't argue, I didn't hand it back, and I didn't say anything! I just put it in my mouth and got ready to light up. I had seen this drill a hundred times with my folks and their friends, and now I was acting just like one of the "cool" grown-ups.

He handed me the lighter. I flicked the little flame on, burning my thumb in the process, and took a deep drag of that delicious acrid tar. I turned green and started hacking, and he started laughing at me. I couldn't really defend myself verbally; I was too busy hacking up a lung. After a moment, I shrugged it off and said, "What? What? I know how to smoke!" I tried to puff on the cigarette a few times without really inhaling because it felt pretty important at that moment not to look any sillier than I already did in front of this guy.

And that's where it began. This guy supplied me for quite a while; we'd meet out back and repeat our drill. He'd offer, and I'd light up. I'm not really sure what was in it for him. Maybe he felt like a "leader" because he was leading me into smoking. As I grew older, I outgrew my need for that guy to be my supplier. I was a pretty big kid, and it wasn't too difficult for me to walk right into the store and buy cigarettes for myself.

It was a while before my mom caught on, and even then, she didn't catch me very often. She threatened to punish me, but she never really followed through with grounding me for smoking—maybe because I was already getting grounded all the time for bad grades in school. I had started to figure out ways to hide the giveaway signs so that

I could sneak around behind my mom's back; for example, I would brush my teeth before I would come home to try to get rid of the smoker's breath.

I wasn't a really serious smoker until the ninth grade, although I did smoke on and off from the sixth grade until then. Smoking was one of my major downfalls in keeping up with football: When your lungs are filled with tar, you have a tough time racing the other guys on the field. By the time I was sixteen, my drinking and smoking had degraded my level of fitness to the point that I couldn't keep up at all on the field, and I would crash and burn at tryouts.

I know how susceptible all of us, especially kids, can be to negative influences. As a dad, it's only prudent of me to figure that at some point, my own kids might be at some sort of get-together with friends, and one of those kids might offer them beer, cigarettes, or worse. I hope it doesn't happen, but I'm not naïve enough to think that it won't. The very best thing I can do is prepare my kids today for the conversation. I teach my kids to say no. I ask them, "What are you going to say if someone hands you a beer?" They answer, "Say no!" We go down the list: alcohol, drugs, or getting into the car with someone they think is under the influence. The answer we practice each time is: "No!" By practicing in advance, they are prepared for what to do and say if they should ever find themselves in that situation. But more than that, I want my kids to understand *why* they should say no. It's not enough for them to be obedient; I want them to be convicted about their decision.

When I look back on all the bad decisions I made as a kid, all the negative stuff I got involved in, I'm surprised to see how far I've come. Who would have thought that a kid who got involved in all sorts of negative situations would ever build a leadership community of tens of thousands of people? It just goes to show that each of us, even me, can change and grow to become the leader he or she is capable of being.

> *I want my kids to understand* why *they should say no. It's not enough for them to be obedient; I want them to be convicted about their decision.*

Grounded for Being "Stupid"

Once you learn to quit, it becomes a habit.[15]

—Vince Lombardi

By the time I was in sixth grade, things had reached a breaking point for me with school. I can honestly say that up until then, I had tried really, really hard to make it work. I would sit at the kitchen table studying for hours. I would feel really confident the night before the test. I had worked hard, paid my dues, and felt that surely I was going to do well. But by the next day, I would blank out. It would all be gone. Everything I had worked so hard on the last few nights would dissolve like dust. I would sit at my desk, staring at the questions on the page in front of me, and think, "I can't believe they are asking me these questions because they don't seem to have anything to do with the book I just read!"

I had convinced myself that I was hopeless. In fact, it was a vicious cycle: The more I failed, the more convinced I was that I was stupid—which had become a self-fulfilling prophecy. I would literally say to myself over and over, "I'm dumb. I'm dumb." I didn't understand it at the time, but I was actually subconsciously programming myself for defeat, making things worse.

Several times throughout that year, my mom was called in to my school to talk to the teachers. No one, including my mom or me, knew what to do. I remember all the teachers telling me, "You're just not applying yourself, Tim." My mom was getting more and more frustrated with me as each report card came home. "You're just not applying yourself, Tim," she echoed. Everyone around me told me I was stupid and lazy. I was getting yelled at pretty much all throughout my time in school.

I remember reaching out for help, and I felt that I was really trying, but the only help I got came in the form of more scolding from teachers and from my mom. Now, this is nothing against my mom—I want to make that very clear. She was a great mom; she was my hero. She was a single woman in the late '70s trying to raise two boys and, at the same time, hold down jobs that would provide for all of us. It's a wonder that she didn't do worse by me.

Just about the only joy in my day during this time was going outside to play. It was like getting a weekend pass out of my jail cell to get a breath of fresh air, get some sunlight, and not be punished for the crime of being the slow kid in class. There was no reading or math to embarrass me, and there were no teachers or parents to scold me and tell me that I was lazy and not applying myself. My buddies didn't judge me that way. We would go outside and ride our bikes, get on our skateboards, and, regrettably, smoke cigarettes. We were always horsing around and having fun, building tree forts, flying kites, and jumping ramps we had built ourselves. I couldn't wait to get out of school and go have fun because it felt as if a huge yoke had been lifted off my shoulders at the end of the day. It was about the only thing I had to look forward to.

So when I really screwed up my marks in the sixth grade, my mom felt like she was at her wit's end as to how to motivate me. With no other obvious options available to her, my mom did what just about every other parent would do; she grounded me. Seems obvious, right? Except that for me, playing outside with my friends was the only light in my day, and now it had been ripped away. School was a constant source of humiliation, and playing was my only release. And now that was gone, too.

Getting grounded was just unbearable for me. My buddies would knock on my door or call me on the phone, and I would have to tell them that I was being grounded "because I'm stupid." That was how I perceived it at the time. My mom said that I would not be allowed to hang out with my friends or do anything fun until my grades improved. And it was about that time, with nothing to look forward to, that I just totally gave up on myself.

I had finally reached and then gone past my tipping point. I threw in the towel and mentally quit on school. I had tried my hardest, and it didn't work. It would be like Shaquille O'Neil trying to be a horse jockey; it just wasn't going to fly. I knew I was just not made for this. I would sit in my room at the end of the day, thinking about how dumb I was, and I would simply leave my books on the counter. Why should I read the homework assignment? I was just going to mess things up anyway, I felt. I already knew that the next day in school, the teacher would yell at me and call me stupid, so why should I make the effort? I just didn't care anymore. I was defeated inside.

So once I had mentally checked out, whatever chance I had of getting passing grades simply evaporated. I managed a perfect year in sixth grade: failing grades in every class. I totally shut down. Why, I even failed gym class. How do you manage that? Well, I don't know how, but I did. I was an absolute, abysmal failure.

I was resigned to my fate. It didn't matter if the teacher yelled at me, and it didn't matter if my mom yelled at me. In my mind, it was all over. I figured that I would *never* get a second chance. I would *never* meet a teacher who would take the time to help me.

But—thank God—I was about to find out that there were still some people who would give me a second chance to redeem myself.

The Little Parochial School That Would

"Chance" is the pseudonym God uses when He does not want to sign His name. [16]

—Anatole France

I ended up going to my dad's house for the summer. The lady I knew at the time as my stepmother (more on that later), bless her heart, had volunteered to put me through summer school and help me catch up on some things. She literally tutored me in math and English, and I managed to get some sort of certificate for having gone through summer school. The grades weren't great, but it was a start.

My mom knew that the situation was looking pretty grim. With failing grades in every class, I was guaranteed to be held back in public school for one year and forced to repeat sixth grade. I had started school a year late, but I was a big kid regardless. Being held back would mean that I would stick out like a sore thumb. I already looked as if I belonged in the eighth grade, and at that age, there was a huge difference. I was smoking cigarettes, and a lot of the other kids were still playing with toys. I was a giant compared to some of them, and the last thing I wanted to be was a head taller than the rest of the class. That would make it pretty easy for the kids to look around and spot the dummy who failed.

So, realizing that the public school system was going to hold me back, my mom started looking at other options. She made some calls, and learned there was a parochial school about fifteen miles away that might be willing to take me – *might* being the operative word. A parochial school was a religious school that was attached to a parish. They weren't likely to be less stern with me, but they also didn't operate under the same academic guidelines as the public schools. There might be some wiggle room.

Through the summer, my mom hatched a plan. She would take that summer school certificate I was earning, show it to the nuns, and resort to a highly advanced negotiating tactic: She would beg. She would beg as though my entire future depended on it, because it probably did.

I remember the drive over there. My mom had a Plymouth Horizon with no air-conditioning, and it was hot outside. I sat in the backseat, and my mom was talking to me throughout the entire drive. She said, "Tim, this is your only shot. You'd better do good here." She explained that she was going to try to talk to the nuns and convince them to admit me into the parochial school. Despite my summer school certificate, I still didn't meet all the requirements that the public school system had set for me to move forward. The nuns were my best shot.

Frankly, I didn't find this to be much of an improvement. I had never been exposed to religion before, and my only image of nuns came from television and movies: They wore habits (their nun uniforms), walked sternly down the rows of seats, and smacked kids on the knuckles with rulers. My only thought was, "I am going to get slapped with a ruler here." My mom figured this environment would help straighten me out. I was terrified.

As we pulled up to the school, we saw a big beautiful Catholic church with magnificent stained-glass windows. Despite the fact that I hadn't had any religion in my life, the sight was pretty awe-inspiring to me. Next to it was a dinky, dingy little building. I remember thinking, "Wow, I hope I never have to go to that place." And my heart sank as we got out of the car and I realized the dingy little building was the school.

I remember going in that small little brick building. It was not very well lit and was kind of a scary place for a kid who has not been exposed to any kind of religion. It even seemed to smell religious, whatever that means. We made our way to the principal's office and walked in to meet her. There were two ladies sitting at the desk. My mom shook their hands and thanked them for seeing us. They said to me, "Okay, we're going to talk to your mom first for a little bit." They told me to sit on a wooden bench in the hallway.

I remember that as I sat outside the office taking in the religious smell, I heard my mom's voice through the door pleading with the school officials. She was saying, "Please, please, just let him come here. I'll do whatever I have to do." I wondered what the heck they were saying to her. They were in there for a good half hour, it seemed. Having never had any exposure to religion, all I kept thinking was that this was not a good situation for me. I imagined that these people were going to do something bad to me because I wasn't being a good kid. I remember feeling judged by these nuns – not that they were judging me; I just felt that way.

Eventually, they called me in. I was scared to death. I felt like a defendant walking into the courtroom after the jury had handed down a verdict. Principal Sister Rita didn't smile at me. She just looked at me and said, "Hi."

The other lady sitting by the desk was a teacher. I learned her name was Sister Judy. She wasn't wearing a traditional nun's habit, but she sure looked like a nun. There wasn't anything glamorous about her. She was dressed in a very conservative brown polyester suit with huge collars that looked homemade. She had very short hair. She was a plump woman with a jowly face, which was glowing. She had a big beautiful smile, and she said, "Hello, Tim." As far as I can remember, it was the first time I ever felt good about a teacher saying my name.

I don't remember everything they said because I was a little numb. I remember bits and pieces. They said they were going to give me a chance. They had decided to accept me into their school. But I was going to have to work hard, and they were going to keep an eye on me.

By the time we got back to the car, my mom looked ten years younger. She was positively thrilled. She was just chattering away in the front seat, talking about how happy she was this had happened, how this was my break, and how I really needed to get to work and pull myself up by my bootstraps. Her biggest relief was that I wasn't going to be held back. But I also knew that with this second chance came an unwanted burden: The parochial school was not publicly funded. My mom was going to have to pay for it out of her own pocket. I couldn't let my mom down. Somehow, I had to make this work. Somehow, I had to figure out how to study and learn and win.

> *I couldn't let my mom down. Somehow, I had to make this work. Somehow, I had to figure out how to study and learn and win.*

YOU ARE FORGIVEN, TIM

Forgiveness does not change the past, but it does enlarge the future.[17]

—Paul Boese

Seventh grade at the parochial school brought all sorts of new pressures to our family. I was well aware my mom was working around two or three jobs, including overtime, and doing everything she could to scrape together the cash to pay for my school tuition. Although I didn't know the exact amount, I knew it wasn't cheap. It was positive pressure for me to do a good job. I didn't want to let my mom down.

Most of the kids who went there were from well-to-do families, so they never had a problem with lunch money. But that wasn't the case for me. I remember another state-funded poor kid named Denny who was on the special lunch program with me. We had to show a card to get food.

Having Sister Judy as my teacher was a whole new experience for me. The biggest change was that — really, for the first time that I could remember — a teacher was being nice to me. She took to me right away. In my mind, a teacher was always someone who yelled at you and put you down, someone who scolded you for not applying yourself, and someone who said, "You got another bad grade, Tim" and "You didn't do your homework again, Tim" – but not Sister Judy. She was totally the opposite. She wasn't a pushover, but she wasn't harsh or belittling to me either. Despite how nice it felt not to be humiliated or attacked, my young brain couldn't handle the contradiction between my negative impression of teachers and her affirming approach with me. One day in class, she must have said or done something that touched a nerve, and that was all the justification I needed to rebel. So early in the year, for a reason that I don't even remember, I decided to believe that Sister Judy was out to get me.

I suppose that I had mentally lumped her in with my past teachers and I was now aiming all my hurt and anger toward them squarely at Sister Judy. It didn't seem to matter that she was the only teacher who had ever been nice to me because, I guess, I had so much baggage stored up in my brain against teachers that I just couldn't see past it all. I decided I would "show her." I would "get her back." All I needed was an accomplice for my devious plan, and that accomplice came in the form of a classmate named Bobby.

Now, Bobby was one of those "special" kids — meaning he definitely had some issues. He had cerebral palsy, and although it was a mild-enough case in that he was still able to walk and talk, it's not a stretch to imagine that he just didn't fit in at school. In fact, no one talked to him; he was the leper of the colony. As it turned out, Bobby lived just right around the block from me, so when I started going to the school, he and I quickly realized we were both the odd man out. We formed an instant bond out of mutual desperation.

It was fall, getting close to Halloween, and the school was having a dance that Friday night. I had arranged with my mom that I would go to the dance and then sleep over at Bobby's house for the weekend.

To really knock this ball out of the park, we needed to start the evening on the right note: We needed to get completely plastered (because all the "cool" kids drink, right?). Our little seventh-grade brains decided we would find someone and convince that person to buy alcohol for us. And find someone we did! We ended up convincing some guy outside the liquor store to buy us a six-pack of beer, a bottle of wine, and a pint of Jack Daniel's. By the end of the night, we had polished off almost all of it between the two of us. We were in seventh grade, and we were completely bombed!

So there we were — totally drunk and raring to go. This, combined with my growing upset feelings toward Sister Judy, was like pouring gasoline on a flame. It created a highly combustible situation. Since I just knew Sister Judy was out to get me, we dreamed up this brilliant idea to get her first. We would egg the school. To a seventh grader, egging the school seemed to be a very sophisticated response to a teacher who was out to get you. We grabbed some eggs and headed out. When I look back on it now, I just shake my head in shame.

So, armed with our bag of ammunition, we walked back to the school. The dance was in full swing by the time we got there, and no one noticed what we were up to outside. We let loose with those eggs and just had a hoot each time they went splat against the windows and brick walls. We ran out of eggs pretty quickly, but we had one final act of vandalism to commit. I reached into our bag and pulled out a big bar of soap. In the biggest letters we could manage, we wrote on the side of the school, "Sister Judy is fat." We thought, "There! That will show her!"

We staggered back into the school to catch a bit of the dance, but as you can imagine, we weren't feeling so great. We called it a night pretty quickly and headed back to Bobby's house to crash. That had been my very first drinking experience. I had gone all out, and my stomach was churning.

Bobby happened to have a *Planet of the Apes* trash can in his bedroom. I will never ever forget that trash can. For the rest of my life, I never want to see anything about the *Planet of the Apes*. I don't want to see the television show, a movie, or even a movie poster depicting it. It instantly brings back memories, and they aren't pleasant ones! That trash can must have been about three gallons, and that night, I filled it to the brim with puke. I barfed my guts out! And not once—no, sir, I filled that ugly *Planet of the Apes* basket three or four times! I totally deserved what was happening to me. (Ironically, the summer of 2011, there was a new *Planet of the Apes* movie in theaters. Hey, guess what? I *was* able to stomach it.)[18]

So there we were: Bobby and I, puking our guts out all night long, and Bobby's mom could hear us! She knew full well what was going on. The next morning, we came down and told her that we weren't feeling so great. It was obvious to anyone who saw us that we were both drunk.

I ended up at my grandparents' house that afternoon, and later that day, my mom came by. We were all sitting around the television when a beer commercial came on. I must have set a new record for the 100-yard dash. I was in that bathroom of theirs at lightning speed; I locked the door and started barfing again. This did not go unnoticed by my family.

When I came out, my mom asked me what was wrong.

I lied to her. "Uh, nothing, Mom. There must be something wrong with my stomach today."

Well, moms have lie detectors for this sort of stuff. She was not at all convinced. She asked me point-blank, "Are you drunk?"

I lied to her again. "No, no, it's just my stomach. I'll be fine."

We headed home, and I suffered through my hangover as the weekend wore on. I told myself I never wanted to drink again. Finally, I got over it by Monday, just in time for the *real* fun to begin.

I was lying in my bed Monday morning, still dozing, when I heard the phone ring. I thought, "That's odd. It's pretty early in the morning to be calling." So I just shrugged and rolled over to go back to sleep. The next thing I knew, my mom was hitting me over the head, yelling, "What did you do! What did you do!"

The phone call had been from Sister Rita. She had summoned my mom and me for an immediate meeting to deal with what Bobby and I had done.

I was surprised by the fact that we had been caught. You see, no one had watched us egg the school. No one had seen us write in soap, "Sister Judy is fat." I thought we had gotten away scot-free! Or so it seemed. The problem was that my accomplice was not the sharpest knife in the drawer. That Friday night, after vandalizing the school, when Bobby and I had wandered back into the building, and while I was off in the bathroom, Bobby took it upon himself to brag to the other kids about the stunt we had just pulled. But he didn't just brag; he said, "I'll show you!" And he took a bunch of kids outside to show them the mess we had made.

When my mom and I arrived at the school, Sister Rita and Sister Judy took us outside to see what Bobby and I had done. We all just stood there looking at it. My mom was seething. I hung my head in shame. Sister Judy was not happy with me. "You're going to clean this up and stay after school in detention."

For the next two weeks, I was in detention. It took us about three days to clean up the walls. Imagine scrubbing off dried egg on coarse brick after it has baked under the sun for a few days. The rest of the time, I would stay after school while Sister Judy marked papers. I would sit at my desk to do the math problems that she had assigned me. I was scared to death to sit in that room with the woman about whom I had written such a mean thing.

But something miraculous happened: She was still nice to me. I couldn't believe it. After all I had done, I was truly stunned that Sister Judy still didn't cast me out. The fact that she showed me grace when I was being wicked and evil was astounding. The incident saw the start of trust building between us and opened the door to our relationship.

It was one of the most crucial turning points of my entire life.

After the two weeks of detention, I remember standing at her desk handing her the last of the detention assignments. She said, "You're a good kid, Tim, and I'm not going to give up on you." And then she came around the desk and gave me a hug. It was the first and only time she had done that. I didn't know what to say. I remember thinking, "Wow, somebody other than my mom actually said something positive to me."

After all I had done, I was truly stunned that Sister Judy still didn't cast me out. The fact that she showed me grace when I was being wicked and evil was astounding.

She kept telling me, "You're going to do better. God's got a plan for all of us, including you, Tim, and I'm not going to let you fail." I remember her saying that to me several times. And so she began to spend hours with me individually. I wish I could say that I completely turned my life around then, but there were still a lot of mistakes I had yet to make, and I still had a lot of growing up to do. But what Sister Judy accomplished was that she opened my eyes to God's love for me and planted in me the seeds of love for God. Even though I didn't understand it at the time, she had opened for me the door toward becoming a man of grace.

After All Those Years, God Reunited Us

I am always amazed, though I should no longer be at this point, at how God works to bless people. Sister Judy had been such a critical part of my childhood, having helped me in ways I can't even measure. But after twenty-plus years, it was not surprising to lose touch with a schoolteacher, even one as influential as Sister Judy.

The story of my connection with Sister Judy, however, does not end with me leaving the parochial school. In fact, I was thirty-six years old when, providentially, we met again. I was a multimillionaire by that time, and Amy and I had gone back to Flint, Michigan, for the funeral of Amy's grandmother. The funeral happened to be held at a school named St. Luke's. It was a run-down little school building, badly in need of a fresh coat of paint and some major renovations. Well, as the funeral was concluding, who should walk into the room but Sister Judy! I couldn't believe it. I hadn't seen her since eighth grade, but I recognized her instantly.

I walked right up to her and gave her a big hug and asked, "Do you remember me?" (I had a lot more hair the last time she had seen me!) She gave me that big glowing smile and said, "Absolutely, I remember you." We chatted, and I learned that she had left the parochial school and was now teaching at St. Luke's. It was great catching up with her. I asked her how things were going at St. Luke's, and I could see that something was troubling her.

"Things aren't going very well here, Tim," she admitted. "The diocese has stopped funding all of the children's programs, so now some of these kids won't be able to stay and will be out on the street. I am so worried for them."

I didn't hesitate. I asked her how much it would cost to fund the program for a year, and she told me. I was shocked at how low the number seemed. "That's all? You're kidding!" I said. I called my assistant and asked her to please bring my checkbook right away. I wrote Sister Judy a check for the total amount for the whole year. I can't tell you how good it felt to do that. She had been such a blessing in my life, and now God had brought us back together on this day so that I could return the gift she had given me and be a blessing in her life. It just felt so good that God allowed me to do that. I know that money ultimately allowed her to positively influence more kids in the same way she had influenced me. I love how God works!

You see, my time in Sister Judy's class had started to change my life. I owed her such a debt of gratitude. I had been with her through seventh and eighth grades, and because of her help, I had started to really turn things around. Under her watchful eye, my grades slowly improved; by the eighth grade, I started getting Cs and Ds, and even a couple of Bs. For someone who got all failing grades in sixth grade, this wasn't just a turnaround — it was a miracle.

I still had to work very hard in class, but the hard work had started to pay off. With my dyslexia still undiagnosed, I was pulling in Ds in English as I struggled with comprehension. But the point is that it was a major step forward. Had it not been for that wonderful woman Sister Judy Berby, I believe that my life would have taken a totally different path. For the first time, things were really looking up. I was blessed to be able to stay at the parochial school all through seventh and eighth grade under Sister Judy's watchful and godly care. And then, as the school year for ninth grade approached, my mom ran out of money.

Despite her best efforts at working two or three jobs at a time to make ends meet for us, my mom just couldn't afford to send me to a private school anymore. There was no other option but for me to go back to the public school system for my first year of high school. Nothing could have been worse for me because I fell in with the wrong kids.

That was when the real trouble started for me. I had merely dabbled in drinking and smoking up until that point when I became a certified expert in the field. With Mom out working all the time to pay the bills, I was left unattended to raise myself. It was as though I was being raised by a pack of wolves in the wilderness, for lack of a better analogy.

All the hard work I had done with Sister Judy to turn my grades around simply unraveled in the space of a year. My grades plummeted, and I was back to earning Ds and worse. I barely scraped through ninth grade. My mom saw how desperate the situation had become, so she borrowed money from my grandparents to send me back to parochial school for the tenth grade. Back in the parochial school, my grades bounced back to Cs and Ds and a B.

It was like a yo-yo: Parochial school, my grades went up; public school, my grades went down. Finally, my mom had begged and borrowed every penny from every family member and every friend who could spare it, and the well eventually ran dry. It was back to public school for good. And without the positive influence of those godly women in my life, all the bad habits came back, hard.

I was back to heavy drinking, and I would drink like a fish until I was thirty. I drank to run away from the pain in my personal life, and I drank to run away from my relationships. I drank to punish myself, and I drank to forget my mistakes. Eventually, I reached a breaking point where I needed to make a very drastic change. And the change came with a threat of divorce, a trip to Florida, and a late-night infomercial promising success.

CONCLUSION

Accept the past for what it was. Acknowledge the present for what it is. Anticipate the future for what it can become.[19]

—Tracy L. McNair

I t might be easy for us to look back on the challenges we had as children and say, "Poor me." We can choose to be limited by the hurts and disappointments, or we can choose to learn and grow. Through the pain I faced, I learned that being a great dad was very important to me. I learned that there were good people in the world, like my mom and Sister Judy, who would fight for me and encourage me. I learned that who you hang around with is going to affect you—for better or worse! And the painful moments we might face in childhood are not entirely needless; they shape us and prepare us to become the best people we can be if we choose to learn the lessons from those experiences.

KEY POINTS

1. We all have defining moments in life. How the moment defines us is our choice. No matter what cards we are dealt,

45

it's up to us to decide how to play them.

2. God hates divorce. It's devastating for the kids.

3. You can't fix a marriage that you leave. Reach out for help and try just a little longer.

4. When my dad stood me up on the day of the canoe trip, I made the decision to become the best dad possible to my future kids. I used the pain of that experience for a positive purpose.

5. The power of association can't be underestimated. If you hang out with people who have bad habits, you will likely soon adopt those bad habits.

6. Sometimes all we need is one person to believe in us in order to turn our lives around. That person can be a family member, a friend, a business associate, or a schoolteacher.

7. Sister Judy forgave me when I was wicked and had treated her badly. Grace toward others can open doors to a relationship.

FROM VIKING TO SUPERMAN

People never improve unless they look to some standard or example higher or better than themselves.[20]

—Tryon Edwards

These days, I have the pleasure of speaking before business audiences across North America. Usually, there is a lot of hoopla and fanfare when people come out onstage to talk, and in order to create a fun presentation, the guys backstage have taken to using theme music for each person as he or she is introduced. I suppose they picked my theme song when everyone learned Amy's nickname for me.

Amy and I have come a long way in our marriage, as I am about to share. It's gotten so good between us that these days, we have pet names for each other that are a little fun and complimentary: I call her Wonder Woman, and Amy calls me Superman. (I call her Wonder Woman because sometimes I wonder why she stuck with me!) Well, I guess my nickname got around when it became the title of a CD I made. But now whenever I walk out onstage, the guys backstage play the theme song to the movie *Superman*.[21]

It's all in good fun, but it's also a little embarrassing. I wonder, "Do these guys not realize what a jerk I used to be, how badly I used to treat people, and how much I still need to grow?" Thankfully, they don't. In fact, I was pleasantly surprised to discover that my younger kids have no memory of Tim "the Viking." They've only ever known the Tim Marks who has been working hard to sand off the offensive parts of his personality.

When Superman transforms into a hero in the movies, he runs into a phone booth to change. I can tell you that I had to go through a process of change just to make it to where I am today, and I am by no means done. Because I had so much work to do to make myself agreeable and pleasant to be around, I buried myself in a positive environment, with uplifting books and CDs and positive people. That environment became a phone booth of sorts so that this unpleasant Viking could grow and change into a better man—someone who, hopefully, inspires people daily.

Define, Learn, Do

Like many people, I never had a teacher take me aside and explain the concept of "define, learn, do." It seems so obvious once you are aware of it, but I'd never heard of this idea being taught in school, and I'd certainly never heard of this at home. The concept is simple enough to explain: We define what we want, learn what is needed to accomplish the goal, and then do what is required to achieve it. The problem for me in my career was that I never did that.

When a kid like me goes through year after year of academic failure, he doesn't always set his career sights very high. I'd given up on school in sixth grade, and I never learned how to figure out what I really wanted. My mom had always told me that I could be anything I wanted to be, but I guess I never really sat down to figure out what that was. A door would open in my life, like a promotion at work, and like many people, I would go through that open door simply because it seemed like the next step forward.

I knew I wanted to get ahead; I just didn't know what that really meant, or how to do it. I also had a couple of major blind spots that I needed to address and a couple of crushing situations that would shape who I was becoming. And each one of these situations helped move me away from the rough-around-the-edges guy that I was and take a step closer to becoming the man I wanted to be. I had a lot of changing to do. I had a lot of rough edges to sand away before I would be able to make a difference in other people's lives. But while I faced all of those issues, I also had a major addiction to break.

And I'm an Alcoholic

Of all the vices, drinking is the most incompatible with greatness.[22]

—Sir Walter Scott

We each find ways of dealing with the pressures of life. Some people hit the race track, hoping for the big win. Others fall to their knees and pray. Some knock over a convenience store, and still others volunteer at a hospital. If my seventh-grade misadventure with Bobby was an indication of anything, it was that I discovered a way to temporarily forget the pressures in my life. Whether it was quitting high-school football or breaking up with my sweetheart, my favorite solution to pain was usually to drink my problem away.

The drinking didn't start as an escape. As with a lot of young guys, it started for me as just a way to fit in with the cool kids. Most of us want to belong to a community, whether it's a church, a gang, a business team, or the clique of cool kids at school. It's scary how a little peer pressure can nudge you in a terrible direction, and I was definitely "nudgeable." That's probably why I believe so strongly in teaching my kids to say no to drugs and alcohol and why I want them hanging around with the right crowd.

Addictions don't begin so obviously; instead, they slip in quietly when we let our guards down and we are weak. For instance, I found that I wasn't a very sociable person, so when I went to a party, it just made it easier if I drank. I'd have a few beers and then a few more. Eventually, it became a real crutch for me. In order to socialize at all, I needed something in my hand all through high school, college, and on into my working life.

> *Addictions don't begin so obviously; instead, they slip in quietly when we let our guards down and we are weak.*

Amy and I actually met and started dating in high school. She had seen me in the hallway when she was in eighth grade, and through mutual friends, we eventually went on a double date and got together. In fact, when my friends first pointed her out to me, I took one look and thought, "That's the girl I'm going to marry." We were sweethearts all through school, and then we broke up and didn't get back together for three years.

More specifically, her parents *made* us break up. Amy was in her senior year at the time, and I was out of high school. (I didn't graduate from high school as you might expect. I had to go to summer school to get my diploma because I was a quarter of a credit shy of what was required. To this day, my high-school diploma has Wite-Out on it hiding the change from "May of 1987" to "August of 1987.") Amy's parents just didn't like some of the things they were seeing in my relationship with Amy. They directed us to part ways and said that if we were truly meant to be together, then eventually, it would happen.

To say that this hit me pretty hard would be an understatement. I was crushed, angry, and bitter, and I felt a little powerless to do anything about it. Her parents wanted me away from their daughter because we both had some growing up to do. Looking back on it, I can see that they definitely made the right decision. Perhaps the way they handled it was a little overbearing, but in hindsight, they were dead accurate.

As I've already mentioned, Amy and I are happily married today, but back then, at the end of high school, my chances of winning her were looking pretty grim. As a young man, I didn't enjoy the luxury of my current hindsight. Back then, I only had right-now sight. I thought Amy was the woman I was supposed to marry, that God had made her for me and me alone. The thought of her dating another guy or being with someone else drove me crazy, so I started drinking even more. And I don't mean I was putting back a six-pack of Coors Light. I was drinking the hardest stuff I could find. A couple of nights a week, I drank 151 proof rum, the stuff you can use to blow flames out of your mouth.

I discovered that repeating this ritual several days a week for six months was starting to have a funny effect on me. More accurately, it started to ruin the lining of my stomach. Before that, I didn't have any problems at all. After this six-month stint, anytime I drank, I would become violently ill. I would vomit so much it was like going through a bout of chemotherapy. My drinking buddies would see how sick I got and say, "Hey, Tim, man, you just need to quit drinking!"

Now, if your drinking buddies are telling you to quit drinking, you have a serious problem! But I wasn't in a teachable mood at the time. So I kept drinking and drinking. I can still remember the many times I would wake up in the morning feeling so sick that I wanted to *die*. This wasn't just a hangover or a headache that a few aspirins might banish—I mean, quite seriously, I wanted to die.

As I was getting into my career, an amazing thing happened in my personal life. One night, I was hanging out at my usual "establishment" when my eyes spotted the most beautiful sight. It was my Amy, there with some friends at the same "establishment." (Okay, okay, it was a bar!) She came over, and we started talking. We both knew that the flame between us had never died.

I ended up giving her a gentleman's ride home that night and dropped her off at her house. She was still living at home with her parents, and she went inside to make the sale of her lifetime to her folks. She explained that we had reunited and wanted to get back together. They could tell she was serious. They listened to her story and said, "All right, all right, you two can date again." A few months later, we got engaged, and about a year later, we were married.

But the drinking continued. I carried on right into my marriage and straight through to fatherhood. When this heavy drinking went on after the birth of my first son Cameron, Amy would have to take Cameron to daycare while I dragged myself out of bed in order to somehow get to a meeting at work.

It would take hours before I could even sip water or eat ice chips because my stomach was so torn up. After a while, the vomiting would stop. Then I'd be pounding back the Rolaids, have a nice cold can of Coke to help soothe the upset tummy, and try to eat some food. I really liked the Burger King fish sandwiches back then. They always seemed to help. Once I could eat a fish sandwich, I was on the road to mending.

So now that my tummy had settled, guess what the plan was for that night? You guessed it: I would go out and start drinking again. I'd get in a few beers, burp a couple of times, and keep on rolling. I would repeat the process every night I could. I would drink till I puked and be sick the next day or two, and as soon as my stomach settled down, I would start drinking again. If my stomach could have handled it, I would have done it every night.

> *I was an alcoholic. I didn't know it, I wouldn't admit it, I couldn't see it, but I was. I told myself I was just a social drinker. I would keep lying to myself for years.*

I was an alcoholic. I didn't know it, I wouldn't admit it, I couldn't see it, but I was. I told myself I was just a social drinker. I would keep lying to myself for years. When someone is getting completely drunk four nights a week (or drinking that much anytime, for that matter), there isn't anything to do but to call a spade a spade.

I had reached the point where I knew something needed to change. At that point in my life, I had finally gone from being "religious" to what the Bible calls in John 3:3 "born again" (ESV). That had really helped put the brakes on a lot of my drinking. I was backing down, doing it more and more rarely. But I would still give in to temptation. Whereas, before I would drink and not care, this time, I would drink and feel guilty. Sadly, it takes a real wake-up call to shock most people into changing for good. And one of those wake-up calls for me was watching my little boy cry.

> *Sadly, it takes a real wake-up call to shock most people into changing for good.*

It was a Sunday morning, and we were supposed to be going to church. I was too sick from drinking to even go. Our bathroom had two doors: one from the master bedroom and one from the hallway. I was running back and forth into the bathroom to vomit so often that I had left both doors wide open. I had thrown up probably five or six times that day. When there was nothing left in my stomach, I dry-heaved, and I didn't even notice the little person standing in the open doorway.

I looked up, and there was little Cameron, three years old, standing in the doorway, crying. He had seen everything, and he was so scared that something bad was happening to his daddy. I remember just sitting back, leaning against the bathtub, and I looked at him and thought, "What in the heck am I doing?"

The pain in my son's face that morning is something I'll never forget and never want to see again. I'd like to tell you I quit after that incident, but there were times after that day when I still gave in to temptation and slipped up. It was another teachable moment to which I didn't pay enough attention.

My path to quitting wasn't perfect, but seeing Cameron cry like that was a real turning point for me. It wasn't until March 29, 2000, that I finally quit drinking. It was a time in my life that was marked by a lot of pressure; I was in the middle of a huge real estate mess and was undergoing terrible stress. And on that day in March, I had my last drink of alcohol, and God delivered me. I haven't had an ounce of alcohol since then. I am still tempted from time to time, but I don't give in to the temptation.

What Can We Do If We Are Struggling to Quit?

My experience through life has convinced me that, while moderation and temperance in all things are commendable and beneficial, abstinence from spirituous liquors is the best safeguard of morals and health.[23]

—Robert E. Lee

If you are struggling with an addiction, as I was for many years, my very first word of friendly advice is this: Don't fool yourself into thinking that you are not an addict, no matter what your addiction is—alcohol, drugs, or pornography. But specifically with regard to alcohol, if you drink to change your state of mind in any way, you need to be concerned that you may have a problem with alcohol.

Today, I am a teetotaler. I try not to be judgmental of those who choose to drink alcohol. However, I do recommend that people examine their motives for drinking. There is nothing biblically wrong with drinking alcohol in itself. The Bible speaks of getting *drunk* as being the sinful behavior. A person commits a sin when he drinks to change his state of mind, or catch a buzz, or calm his nerves. For many people, one beer would be enough to cross that line.

What we do as alcoholics is justify our behavior. We lie to ourselves and say, "I can handle it. I'm only a social drinker." If people could handle it, we wouldn't be faced with the alarming record of drunk driving incidents and the number of senseless fatalities that happen each year. It just causes so much pain and anguish for families. There are many more alcoholics than those who care to admit it because they don't want to give it up. They don't want to give up the good feelings that alcohol brings, even though those feelings are false and empty.

There is other fulfillment in life that is true fulfillment, and you don't need to drown your sorrows in alcohol to find it.

Let me just say this: There is other

54

fulfillment in life that is true fulfillment, and you don't need to drown your sorrows in alcohol to find it. If you told me, "Tim, I know I need to stop, but I am struggling to change," and you asked me what I would recommend, I would say that if you are a Christian, you should pray and ask God to deliver you. Reach out to your pastor. He should be able to give you some materials that will help you make some changes.

Alcoholics Anonymous is a good way to go, regardless of your faith. In the interest of full disclosure, I have not personally been through AA, although I did study it. I agree with what I know about it, including the accountability partners, having someone to talk to when you're struggling, and especially the requirement that you must admit you are an alcoholic. Most people don't have the courage to face reality, and I believe it is a very powerful first step to stand up before a group and say, "Hi, my name is So-and-So, and I'm an alcoholic."

I can't say for sure if I ever said the words "I am an alcoholic," but I certainly admitted to myself that I had a problem with drinking and I needed to stop. It took me a solid month after I stopped to even say the words out loud. People want to avoid admitting it, I believe, because they are embarrassed. Maybe there is a stereotypical view of alcoholics, and we picture a wino laying in the gutter. We might think an alcoholic is someone who smells like vomit and booze, who has a big nose with purple veins, who has been on a six-week bender, and has lost his job and home. But alcoholics are also people like you and me. Half of the time, you can't even tell by looking at them! They look normal, drive a nice car, drop their kids off at a private school, and then hit the bottle behind closed doors. It's like with someone addicted to Internet pornography: You'd never know it by looking at them. They wear a suit, own a business, and have a family. They look good on the outside, but they are hiding this addiction behind closed doors. People want to keep their problems hidden because they are embarrassed; they don't know how to stop. That's why the first step in the AA program is admitting that there is a problem.

You can't get better unless you admit you have a problem.

You can't get better unless you admit you have a problem.

If you are struggling, or think that you might have a problem, I hope you can see the pain it caused me in my own life. I hope my story will encourage you to reach out to a pastor, a friend, or to AA and simply say, "I think I may have a problem, and I'm just looking to talk." It could be a turning point in your life.

GOOD-BYE, MOM

My mother said to me, "If you become a soldier, you'll be a general; if you become a monk, you'll end up as the pope." Instead, I became a painter and wound up as Picasso.[24]

—Pablo Picasso

My mom was my hero, plain and simple. The older I get, and as I look back on how she played the hand she was dealt, the more amazed I am that she was even able to put food on the table for us. I now understand what it took for her to wake up in the morning and go to work at the bank during the day, while arranging for me to have somewhere to go after school—usually at the house of a friend. Once, she even cajoled someone into getting me to football practice. She was an expert at juggling.

I remember my mom being stressed out over our finances because my dad didn't send her child support, or he sent her only a portion of it. So every moment she could, my mom worked. She would race home and then head off to her second job, where she worked all night at a hospital. Then she spent the weekends working at a bingo hall. She scraped together what pennies she could find to make the mortgage payment, keep the lights on and the water running, and put some food in the fridge. Sometimes the pickings got pretty slim, but I never remember going to the fridge and not finding something

I could eat. (My uncle worked for General Mills, so he was able to get us cereal.)

My mom was literally the caregiver, the sole parental example, and the leader of the house. Through all that she did, she still made time on occasion to take me outside and throw a football around with me. Not often, but enough times that I have a memory of her doing it. She just knew a teenage boy needed a parent to play catch with him. She didn't know a darn thing about throwing a football, but God bless her, she did her best.

My mom never really read a book on leadership or self-development, but she still managed to hammer some strong values into my brother and me. "Don't lie. Do what you say you are going to do." And one of the most important things for me was that she believed I could do whatever I dreamed of doing. She would say, "You can be whatever you want to be. If you want to be the president, if you want to be an engineer, if you want to be an NFL football player, you can do it. Don't let anybody tell you anything different." Those were pretty powerful words coming from a woman who had been beaten down by circumstances her whole life.

> *"You can be whatever you want to be. If you want to be the president, if you want to be an engineer, if you want to be an NFL football player, you can do it. Don't let anybody tell you anything different."*

Getting divorced in the early '70s was definitely not a chic thing to do like it is today, with 50 percent of couples now doing it. Although I didn't see a lot of it, I'm aware she probably faced a real social backlash because of her family situation. And yet, despite the social stigma and the financial stress, my mom kept up a pretty positive attitude. She taught me more through her example than by her words to have a positive outlook in life and not to focus on the negative. She always found a way. She always found a car to drive, a job to make the mortgage payment, a coupon to clip so she could feed her boys for another week. It was inspiring to me, and still is, to see how much she did with how little she had.

It's no surprise, then, that she battled depression and that she didn't always make the best choices in dealing with things. My mom wasn't perfect by any stretch. There were times when the stress she was under showed in the way she treated us, and sometimes she was unfairly harsh with us. She didn't have anyone to help her, but she tried her best, even though she did lash out at us at times. She also turned to drinking, which, I'm sure, paved the way for my own drinking problems later on. I saw my mom get drunk many times, and she thought that it was perfectly fine and normal. It was one of her ways of dealing with things, although it was a bad choice.

She wasn't perfect; no parent is. I'm not perfect, and neither is Amy (although she's pretty close!). My mom admitted to me in later years that she wished she had done a better job as a parent. She was pretty hard on herself and felt she had really let us down. She said, "I could have done things differently. I wish I hadn't been so angry." But here's how I know that she did a good job as a parent: I look back more on all of the positive things she taught me in my life instead of all the negative things that she did to me.

So many parents question themselves, just as my mom did. My mom did a better job than I can even put into words. Just the fact that we never ended up in jail speaks to the fact that my mom put enough of a moral compass in us to keep us on track. Even though the moral compass didn't have a true north and needed to be tapped every once in a while to make sure it was still working, there was still enough direction to know that acts such as stealing were wrong.

> I'll bet you're doing a better job at being a mom or a dad than you give yourself credit for. Just because you think you've made mistakes, that doesn't make you a bad parent. Your kids can still turn out great.

So I'd like to make this point to any single mom or dad who might be reading this book: I'll bet you're doing a better job at being a mom or a dad than you give yourself credit for. Just because you think you've made mistakes, that doesn't make you a bad parent. Your kids can still turn out great.

The Phone Call

Tragedy tends to wake us up to what's really important in our lives. I didn't realize how precious my mom really was to me until I returned home from work one day, only to find a message waiting for me on the answering machine. It was my mom. She had gone to the

> *Tragedy tends to wake us up to what's really important in our lives.*

doctor that day to have her chronic sore throat checked and had received some very unexpected and somber news. That phone call to me was the kind of call that you can't ever prepare for, but one that you know will eventually come.

"Tim, it's Mom. I need to talk to you . . . I just found out that I have cancer . . . Call me back." Well, I didn't return her call; I drove to her house right away.

We arranged to meet with her doctor. I had never faced a situation like this; all of this medical stuff was brand new to me. The doctor walked us through what to expect, what the options were, and what her chances were. We decided we would fight it. If someone else had beaten this, then it was possible my mom could beat it. We were going to fight it, and we were going to win. And my mom fought very, very hard for a long time.

Thus began almost a year of chemotherapy—eleven months, to be exact. The one saving grace for my mom during those months was that we finally had Cam. My little guy was the light of Mom's life, as she had wanted a little grandchild to hold for so long and was always pressuring Amy and me to get busy with starting a family. I'm so glad we had Cameron when we did because it meant so much to Mom to be able to hold that beautiful little boy in her arms. My mom loved Cam more than anything, and she would do anything for him. I think that just getting to hold him gave her extra strength to hang on a little while longer. It probably added months to her life.

With her options dwindling, my mom figured she had one chance left: a bone marrow transplant. It was a really risky procedure because,

59

basically, they kill all of the bone marrow in your body, essentially killing you, and try to put the marrow from a donor into you; then you pray that it takes. If not, then that's the end. The doctors were pretty clear that without this procedure, she would be gone in a few months, but her quality of life in the final few months would be tolerable. The transplant would be a horrible experience for anyone going through it, but if it worked, it meant she would live. I felt really uncomfortable about the risks, but it was my mom's choice. And she chose to fight to live using any means necessary. She chose to do the bone marrow transplant.

This meant isolating her because of the high risk of fatal infection. And that meant that she couldn't see Cameron anymore. The doctors were clear that the only way she would see Cam was either when she was released from the hospital or if the procedure failed. If she was about to die, she would have nothing to lose. And the prospect of no longer being able to hold a baby grandson would be really tough for any grandparent to handle.

In my mother's final two months, I would drive down to Harper University Hospital in Detroit, an hour each way, to see her. I don't know if you've ever known anyone who had to go through something like this, but there is almost no way to prepare for it. Walking in there each day was a ritual that I would prefer to forget. I remember having to scrub up and put on a gown and a mask before I went into her room. I will never ever forget the smell of sterile hospital cleaning solution. Every time I go into a hospital today, as soon as that smell hits me, it takes me right back to those times in the cancer ward with my mom. That's why I hate hospitals to this day. I never want to smell that smell again.

In fact, the whole experience just stuck with me. Little things that were no big deal started to really get to me. For example, the cafeteria served only Wendy's burgers. No big deal, right? Up until then, I enjoyed Wendy's like a lot of people. But each day, I would visit my sick mom and then eat at Wendy's – visit my mom, and then eat at Wendy's. After the hospital, I couldn't touch any Wendy's food for a year. One bite of a Wendy's burger just brought back way too many bad memories.

Although I can't stand to go into hospitals to this day, I will do so if there is a friend or a family member whom I need to see. Obviously, I won't deny them my support and my presence just because of my baggage. That would be incredibly selfish of me. I know some people who give in to this kind of selfishness and won't go to a hospital or to a funeral. I sure hope that if I was in the hospital, my friends and my family would come to see me.

Each time I would walk into my mom's room at Harper, I would get this sick feeling in my stomach, wondering, "How bad is she going to be today?" Sometimes she'd be sleeping, and sometimes she'd be looking out the window. I remember one time in particular after a round of chemo: She literally had blood pooling up in the corners of her eyes. A few of the little blood vessels in her eyes had popped, and it just broke me inside to see her like that. I remember this terrible uncertainty in me. One minute I would argue with myself, "Why did I ever let her choose to do this?" And then the next moment, I would wonder how I would feel if she hadn't tried and then we had lost her. I'd have to carry that guilt for the rest of my life.

I felt a sense of responsibility that she was going through all of that. Knowing what I know today about homeopathic methods, I would never have put my mom through that procedure; I would have explored a natural route because I have seen firsthand what some expert homeopathic practitioners have done to help my immediate family. I believe if we had gone the homeopathic route, things would have turned out differently for her. I know that many people have gone through a bone marrow transplant successfully, so there is definite value in that remedy as well. I believe there will eventually be a cure for cancer that is shared with people around the world.

However, what happened to my mom was part of God's plan. Romans 8:28 says, "And we know that for those who love God all things work together for good, for those who are called according to His purpose" (ESV). As hard as it

> *Many things that happen are not good, but they are a part of God's plan.*

might be for us to face, many things that happen are not good, but they are a part of God's plan.

The Letter

It soon became apparent that the bone marrow transplant was not working. There was no need to quarantine Mom from holding Cameron anymore; it was obvious that she only had a few precious days left with us. I will always remember taking Cam in that last time for Mom to hold. She was barely speaking that day and was basically in a coma. She was shaking, but she managed to hold him as best as she could and told him, "Grandma loves you, Cam." He was seven months old at the time—too young to ever have a memory of her. She just looked at me after that, and her eyes said everything. She knew it was almost over.

The last week of my mom's life, I stayed with her the whole time. I watched her get down to two respirations a minute. It was a little surreal. We kept thinking she had passed, and then she would gasp for air. The nurses were giving her such heavy doses of morphine that I think they were trying to let her die from a morphine overdose, but it just didn't happen. I was thinking, "Mom, please just go. You don't have to wait."

There were three of us in the room when the nurse came in for the final time. She said, "You know, some people just won't die with people in the room." And so, we prayed with Mom, talked with her, and told her we loved her. I told her we would be okay and that she could go. And we walked out. I know she was thinking, "I don't want to die in front of my kids. It will hurt them too badly." That's just how my mom was. She didn't want to put anyone out. The nurse was right; in just a few minutes, she was gone.

After it happened, I thought, "How selfish am I for staying with her in the room? She was laboring to stay alive for *me*, and if I had left earlier, it might have made things easy for her."

When we got home, we found a letter waiting for us. The cover said, "If you get this letter, I must already be gone." Mom figured that undergoing this procedure might do her in, so she wanted to make sure she got her thoughts down on paper while she still had a chance. Her letter read,

Tim, I love you. Amy, I love you as if you were my own daughter. Cam, you will never know how much Grandma loves you. Your dad and mom will just have to tell you. Tim, take extra good care of Cam. He is a bright, strong, and special boy. He is going to grow up to be someone special, not only in our lives, but in the lives of so many people.

Tim, I'm so proud of you and the way that you turned out. You're a very loving, caring, and compassionate man. You were that way as a boy, too. Take good care of Amy. You can tell Cam Grandma is his guardian angel. Remember, John is your brother, your only brother, so don't lose contact. Amy, take care of Tim and Cam for me.

I love you all very much,

Mom

My first thought when I read the letter was that I didn't appreciate her enough while she was here. My mom loved life and loved people. She loved Amy even more than she loved me. She loved Cam more than he will know. I truly believe that she lived those extra months just to see a little more of her grandson. He had just been born when she was going in and out of the hospital. She would literally go home from the hospital after chemotherapy and make us bring him over. She would stay up with him all night, hugging and kissing him.

In those final eleven months, I started to realize how precious every moment we have with our loved ones

If you are fortunate enough to still have your parents here, I'd like to encourage you, as the Bible says, to "honor your father and your mother" and treasure every moment you have together.

can be. A good friend and business partner of mine celebrates every Friday by spending the day with his dad. Whether they are working on his basement or going fishing, my friend and his dad are creating wonderful memories together. If you are fortunate enough to still have your parents here, I'd like to encourage you, as the Bible says, to "honor your father and your mother" (Exodus 20:12, ESV) and treasure every moment you have together.

ENTERING THE RAT RACE

The trouble with life in the fast lane is that you get to the other end in an awful hurry.[25]

—John Jensen

Coming out of school, I wasn't exactly gearing up for a white-collar career. With my marks, I pretty much figured I was going to be using my hands instead of my head in order to make money. And so I started out as a laborer and soon became a welder.

As I mentioned before, my dad didn't help out much financially while we were growing up. Not many pennies of alimony or child support ever made their way into my mom's hands. I saw the financial pressure she was always under as she tried to make ends meet on her own. Because of that, it was very clear in my head that my job as the man of the house was to put a roof over our heads and food on the table, and I swore I was going to do that. What the other guys in school might have over me in the way of book smarts, I had over them when it came to elbow

What the other guys in school might have over me in the way of book smarts, I had over them when it came to elbow grease. I could roll up my sleeves and outwork anyone.

grease. I could roll up my sleeves and outwork anyone. And outwork them I did.

I started working eighty to ninety hours a week. I would travel for work, sometimes even being away for a week at a time. It doesn't take a rocket scientist to figure out that this kind of schedule would start to create some tension at home. But I wouldn't hear of it; I didn't want to listen. I just put my head down and worked.

Amy and I had some deep-rooted marital issues that we were avoiding, which ended up taking us years to work out. Additionally, Amy reminded me of my mom, which caused me tremendous pain. Put all that together with my work schedule, and you have a recipe for disaster.

When Amy looked for support, her family actually took *my* side, telling her, "At least you've got a husband who's willing to work so hard to provide for you!" But Amy felt abandoned. She didn't care what house we lived in or what car we drove; she married me to be with *me*, not to be alone. She just wanted her husband home. And yet this crazy lifestyle went on—not for a few weeks or months, but for *years*.

With my kind of work ethic, it was no surprise I shot up through the ranks pretty quickly at work. I went from being a welder to being a supervisor. I started to outgrow the first manufacturing company where I worked and moved on to another company to assume the responsibilities of a maintenance supervisor.

One day at the new company, I was bending some conduit, which was a very hot and tedious job. I noticed one guy standing off to the side drinking some coffee. He looked pretty comfortable while I was sweating. I asked my journeyman, "What does that guy do?"

He answered, "Well, that guy is an engineer!"

Immediately, I had a new and very clear goal. I decided that standing around drinking coffee was better than bending pipe. So I decided right there that I wanted to be an engineer. That's about as complicated as making a life-altering decision could get.

There was one small hurdle, however: Being an engineer meant going to college, and I was no good at school. Remember, I was "dumb." I couldn't read properly, I struggled with ADD and dyslexia, and I had gotten Cs and Ds during my best times. I graduated from high school with a GPA of 1.8, for heaven's sake! How in the world was I going to pull this off?

The answer involved swallowing some pride and admitting my weakness, but not letting this obstacle beat me. There was a kid working for me at the time, probably nineteen years old, whom I took aside one day and made an offer that he couldn't refuse. I invited him to become my tutor after work. Now, mine was not a very well-paying job, and it wasn't very glamorous work. However, I had a little negotiating power: This kid was my employee, and I was his boss. I had a very straightforward conversation with the young man, and we had a clear understanding as to what he was going to be doing two nights a week. I offered him eight dollars an hour, and we were off to the races.

The workload for the next few years was pretty brutal. I was already working sixty to seventy hours a week at my job, and now I had added college. I went to night school three nights a week for over three years, and I spent another two nights a week studying with my tutor. Hiring a tutor was one of the smartest moves I made. It did make for a strange relationship with this kid because I was his boss during the day, and yet there he was at night, explaining to me what must have been some pretty simple stuff for him. It was a little humbling for me to ask for help, but I was too determined to pass those tests to let my big ego get in the way. Juggling all of these hats and working all of these hours created some very real stress for me.

Whenever I was home, I was studying. Amy and I were arguing all the time about my schedule, and I was forever explaining to her that I was doing all of this to provide for us and to get ahead. I honestly believed at that point, as a lot of folks do, that one has to have a degree to make it in this world. Obviously, I know better now, but back then, I didn't understand the difference between having a piece of sheepskin on the

> *I didn't understand the difference between having a piece of sheepskin on the wall and having some real-world wisdom you can use to create wealth.*

wall and having some real-world wisdom you can use to create wealth.

It should have been a tip-off when I realized that my college instructor was a GM engineer working nights teaching in order to scrape together a couple extra bucks. Here was this guy being paid to teach us quadratic equations, and I quickly realized he was on the same career path as me, only twenty years ahead. He was an engineer who was not making enough money, and I was studying under him, about to follow in his footsteps! When I look back on it, I chuckle at the irony of the situation.

Back then, I at least saw that a lot of what he was teaching was a big waste of time. I would challenge him from time to time, asking, "When are we ever going to use that equation that you've just taught?"

He would pause for a moment, think about it, and finally say, "Tim, in twenty-five years at GM, I have never used that equation once." And then he would go back to teaching it! Higher education isn't always that smart. But I was determined to study and move on to the next level because that was what my job was asking of me.

While I was making my way through college, I must have been doing something right, because I got a phone call from a recruiter who offered me a job at a large automotive supply company. It really was a prestigious place to work, I felt, compared to the other jobs I had had before. The company offered great benefits and a great salary. Everyone seemed to be fighting just to get in the door, and I caught the bug as well. I decided I wanted the job. In fact, I chose to take a second-shift job as a maintenance supervisor there just to get my foot in the door.

The week I started my new job was the same week my mom died. My boss was very understanding, and he let me start a week later so I could arrange the funeral and take care of family matters.

While the management at this new workplace seemed great, my new schedule was not. Working second shift was an absolute nightmare. It ended up being pretty much around the clock. My body just couldn't take it, but I stuck with it for two months. After that, I went to my boss and said, "This isn't going to work. I never see my wife anymore." I was pretty convincing, so they gave me a job on first shift.

What happened next really opened my eyes to how brutal corporate America can be. After about four months on the job, I was working so hard that I was really getting a lot done, perhaps more than the other people around me. Because of this, a few of the higher-ups sat me down one day and said, "We're promoting you." This sounded great, except I realized what was going to happen was that my boss would be pushed aside and I would be handed his job.

I felt horrible about this. I didn't want my boss's job, especially in light of him being treated so badly. I told them I would rather just leave. Now they went into damage-control mode. They brought my boss, the plant manager, and me together in a room and said, "Well, Tim, we were going to move your boss anyway. We are going to find someone to take the job, and we'd like it to be you."

My boss turned to me and said, "I knew the day I hired you that I was hiring my replacement." It was such a lesson to me that we, the employees, were just a number to management. I went along with it and accepted the job. I am all for the performer getting the promotion, but the way it went down was just wrong.

The next three years were a blur, with me continuing to receive promotions, making my way up through the ranks and, eventually, into the engineering department. While my career was taking off, my marriage was tanking.

Amy and I were literally passing each other like ships in the night. We would see each other for maybe two hours every other day. Some days I wouldn't see her or Cameron at all. I would wake up at four thirty in the morning, leave for work, and arrive at the plant at five fifteen. Many nights, I wouldn't be home until nine or ten o'clock in the evening. This was the case six or seven days a week for three years.

I was a success at work but a failure at home. I didn't have a healthy marriage, and I wasn't being a good dad. But on the outside, I looked like I was winning in life. I wouldn't listen to anyone else; I took only my own advice. It wasn't until I discovered the tapes of a motivational guru with a Southern drawl that things began to make a turn for the better.

Zig Ziglar

I believe that being successful means having a balance of success stories across the many areas of your life. You can't truly be considered successful in your business life if your home life is in shambles.[26]

—Zig Ziglar

My whole goal at that point in my life was to be a plant manager for the automotive supply company. My goal wasn't to be a good father, a good husband, or a good family man; it wasn't to do what was *right*—it was to be a plant manager, and that was all. And in my mind, Amy's job was to take care of the family. To say my priorities were out of whack would have been an understatement.

Because I was being fast-tracked on an LDP, or leadership development plan, my employer paid to fly me to a management seminar. Once the seminar started, I knew pretty quickly that the instructor didn't have a clue what he was talking about. He was suggesting a whole lot of ridiculous things, such as, "You should listen to your people." Any stubborn and delusional Viking will tell you that you shouldn't listen to your staff—you should just attack them and make them feel bad (which, by the way, was a big part of why I was such a bad manager for my staff back then)!

The seminar leader even quoted John Maxwell's *The 21 Irrefutable Laws of Leadership* and the law of buy-in.[27] I remember being so full of myself, so ignorant as to how to lead people, that I was openly disagreeing with most of what they taught that day. A couple of times, they said something I felt was worth writing down, but mostly, I was just dismissive.

At the seminar, they had a store where you could buy some sales and management aids. On the table was a tape set labeled *Goals* by a motivational speaker and author named Zig Ziglar. The name sounded familiar to me, so I was intrigued. Since I arrogantly thought that I had already mastered goal-setting but my staff had not, I thought the tape set would be a great teaching aid for *them*. I plunked down my thirty dollars and started listening to the tapes.

The first thing that struck me about Zig was his accent. He was living in Dallas, Texas, but he grew up in Yazoo City, Mississippi, so he had a pretty deep Southern drawl. And I couldn't stand the sound of his voice. I automatically judged him, thinking, "This guy is some sort of country bumpkin. I can't believe I wasted my money on these tapes!" I was so irritated I almost—*almost*—pulled the tape out and threw the set away. I was that offended. But something made me keep listening, and I believe it was God.

Within twenty-five minutes, I went from being offended by Zig's accent to falling in love with the guy. I thought, "Wow, this guy is speaking the truth." He started talking about values and having one's priorities in line. And it was the first time I ever remember thinking there was an outside possibility I didn't have life totally figured out.

I was hooked. I bought some more of his tapes and then discovered and bought some more. In the mid-1990s, I bought every recording from Zig Ziglar that I could get my hands on. I became a Zig Ziglar nut. I studied his tapes so much I could quote them. And miraculously, on one of the flyers that came with a Zig Ziglar tape, I discovered he had a series called *Christian Motivation for Daily Living*. That appealed to me because I had started going back to church, and I thought, "Hey, I'm a Christian." I figured that by doing those things, I was automatically a Christian. I decided to buy those tapes as well.

Listening to Zig's religious beliefs was harder at first than listening to his accent, to be honest. He was a Baptist, and I had been raised to believe that Baptists were just weird. I was used to going to a church that was full of all kinds of traditions and works but very little grace. I assumed I was a Christian simply because I lived in the United States and went to church. That's like thinking that if you sit in a garage, it will automatically make you a car. Just as it would take a miracle for you to simply become a car, it takes a miracle for us to become Christians.

Zig talked about the plan of salvation. That concept was totally foreign to me. I always thought you just needed to believe in God, be a good person, read your Bible, and pray. I figured that was all that was needed to be right with God. And Zig said that wasn't enough!

He then shared a verse that totally changed my life. It was Ephesians 2:8–9. I was on I-69, headed for Woodbridge, Canada, when I heard him quote the passage. It made such an impact that the first chance I got, I actually pulled out a Bible to look up the verse and study it.

It reads, "For it is by grace you have been saved through faith. And this is not your own doing; it is the gift of God, not a result of works, so that no one may boast" (ESV).

For the first time in my life, I felt, "Uh-oh, I am a sinner. I have sinned. And I cannot get to heaven because of this sin. I need a Savior to get to heaven."

> *For it is by grace you have been saved through faith. And this is not your own doing; it is the gift of God, not a result of works, so that no one may boast.* – *Ephesians 2:8–9 (ESV)*

I did not know at the time how to receive Jesus Christ as my Lord and Savior, but I knew something was happening to me. I knew that the God of the Universe was after me, and I praise Him for that. I learned that Zig was speaking at a big motivational conference about two months later in Auburn Hills, Michigan, and I had the opportunity to go. The promo said that anyone who bought one of Zig's books would have the opportunity to have him sign it.

Well, I was so broke at the time that I didn't even have the money to buy a book. What I did have, however, was my affirmation card that came in one of the tape packs. I figured, "That'll do!" I stood in line and finally got my chance to meet Zig. I got to shake his hand, and he gladly signed my affirmation card. He signed it Ephesians 2:8–9. I laminated it, and I still have it today. That was the verse God used to save me, and I became right with God. I credit Zig Ziglar with being the instrument that God used.

Thou Shalt Not Commit Adultery

But Zig wasn't done with me yet. In addition to opening my eyes to my need for salvation, he opened my eyes to my failing marriage. It was a story on Zig's tapes that hit me like a wrecking ball. The story was about a young man who was working himself half to death and whose family never saw him. A wealthy older friend of the young man had written a letter to Zig:

> *Mr. Ziglar, I know a young man who needs your help. I know you don't do counseling, but here is a check in advance for your time. If you could spare an hour in your schedule for my young friend, I know you could have a positive impact in his life.*[28]

Zig replied, "You're right. I don't do counseling, so here's your check back. But I am willing to give you and your young friend an hour of my time, free of charge. Bring this young man down to Dallas. I am happy to talk with him, and if I can help him, I will."[29]

The arrangements were made, and soon thereafter, the young man was sitting across the table from Zig. "So," Zig asked the young man, "do you consider yourself a success?"[30]

"Absolutely," the young man answered.[31]

"Why are you successful?" Zig asked.[32]

Without hesitating, the young man said "Because I'm doing what my boss does."[33]

Zig wondered why the young man thought his boss had it made. The young man explained that his boss was very successful because he worked a lot of hours, had a lot of responsibilities, and made a lot of money. Zig nodded and asked about the boss's family life.[34]

"He's divorced," came the reply.[35]

"What about his kids?" Zig wondered.[36]

"They don't really like him," answered the young man.[37]

Zig paused and asked a final question: "Does it seem like he's a happy man?"[38]

"Well, I've never seen him smile," answered the young man.[39]

I remember that as Zig patiently and gently went down a laundry list of all the qualities of a successful life, with the young man answering quite negatively about his boss on each point, I felt *numb* – absolutely numb. I thought, "Uh-oh, I'm that guy that he's talking about."[40]

Even though I had achieved more success in corporate America at that point than I would have ever imagined, I felt like a loser. I was being fast-tracked through the leadership development program and was being groomed to become a plant manager. I was twenty-seven, and I was on top of the world at work. But I felt lower than a snake's belly at home. I finally realized that, as the Scriptures describe it, I was grasping for the wind.

I realized I was committing adultery, but not in the way you might think I mean. I had been having an affair with my *job*. I was cheating on my wife by working late and loving my career more than her. From that day forward, I vowed to figure a way out of the mess we were in. I sat in my car thinking about Amy and how badly I was messing things up at

> *I realized I was committing adultery, but not in the way you might think I mean. I had been having an affair with my job. I was cheating on my wife by working late and loving my career more than her.*

home. I thought, "Here's Amy, the girl I've loved since I was a senior in high school, the girl I had always dreamed of marrying, and here I am, ignoring her." I wasn't loving her, I wasn't spending time with her, and I wasn't cherishing her as I said I would in our marriage vows. I had promised, "for better or worse," and a lot of it had been "for worse." And something was about to change.

WE'RE LEAVING, TIM

You can never be happily married to another until you get a divorce from yourself. A successful marriage demands a certain death to self.[41]

—Jerry W. McCant

I once heard someone say, "The opposite of love isn't hate; it's indifference." For years, I had shown Amy nothing but indifference, and it was only time before I eventually wore her down. For years, I would come home exhausted, plunk down on the couch to watch TV, and then pass out. Amy wanted to spend time with me, but I would brush her off, explaining that I had worked hard all day. I told her I had to work all these hours in order for us to have the nice lifestyle we enjoyed. Cameron was usually in bed asleep by then. He was our only child at that time, so I really wasn't even a part of the family.

> The opposite of love isn't hate; it's indifference.

My relationship with Amy had become bitter and cold—colder than a tin toilet seat on the shady side of an iceberg! It was as sterile as my mom's hospital room. There was almost zero love. We were just corporate partners, splitting the bills. One time, Amy actually said, "Tim, you're just a paycheck to me." That was how empty things had become between us. The girl that I was once madly in love with, or so I had thought, was now just a roommate. And she finally had had enough.

It was a Sunday night when I pulled up to find her bags packed at the back door. She had Cameron in one hand and her bags in the other. I asked, "Where are you going?"

And she said, "I'm going to my mom and dad's."

I asked, "When are you coming back?"

And she answered coldly, "I'm not."

I felt as if I had been punched in the gut. I knew our marriage was on the verge of ending that night and that I had let it erode to nothing. I broke down crying right there in the doorway and begged her to stay. I told her I would change; I told her I would do whatever it took. And she told me I had said it all before but nothing ever changed. But by some miracle, some shred of forgiveness, maturity, or grace on Amy's part gave her the strength to put her bags down and take Cameron back to his bed to sleep on it for another night. And providentially, that was the week that we had already scheduled a family vacation in Florida.

The Florida Trip and the Rowboat

The very week Amy had packed her bags and threatened to leave, my boss had brought me in to his office to let me know I was up for yet another promotion. I was to be the head of all engineering, overseeing all sorts of maintenance, robotics, tooling, facilities—the works! And I was only twenty-nine years old. This was unheard of in corporate America. I was flattered, but in my gut, I knew my life was not on track. I knew, even before the night Amy threatened to leave, that I had to make a change. For the first time, I didn't accept the promotion right away. But I didn't turn it down right away either.

Listening to the Zig Ziglar tapes had not only helped me rekindle my faith and start thinking about my family life, but it had also made me think about leaving my job. I started wondering whether there was a better way. And now that my antennas were up, I started noticing things I had been ignoring before. I started seeing opportunities that had always been in front of me. One late-night infomercial that caught my attention gave me the idea of owning rental properties. I started thinking that if I could buy enough rental properties, I could generate a sufficient income to be able to leave my job so I could have time at home with Amy and Cam.

The Florida trip came about because I had won a contest at work. Whoever saved the plant millions of dollars got to take the trip south with his spouse, and there was a real competition to get that trip. I won along with three other guys. Our reward was two days in Florida, sitting in business meetings. I figured it would be a good idea to stretch the trip out by a few days and take some family time. And the timing was perfect.

Once I got through the meetings in Orlando, the first thing Amy and I did was rent a rowboat. We rowed around this beautiful pond, just Amy and Cameron and me. I couldn't remember the last time that all of us were together with no phones ringing and no other interruptions – just the three of us together as a family, talking and enjoying each other's company.

I have to admit that at first it felt a little strange. I was a little out of practice just hanging out. I remember looking at Amy and Cameron and thinking, "Wow! This is my family. This is *my* family." And in that little rowboat on that Orlando pond, I fell in love with Amy all over again. I fell in love with my family and wanted to be with them. To this day, whenever I'm in Orlando, I drive by that pond and think, 'That's where we took the rowboat out."

I decided I wanted to see how the other half lived, so, on a whim, I rented a Cadillac. We drove around Florida in that car for a week, and I enjoyed it very much. I loved the feel of the drive and the smell of the leather, and I said, "Wow, honey, could you ever imagine having a brand-new Cadillac that smells just like this?" We drove down to the area where we live now, walked around, and saw all the touristy things Florida has to offer.

During that week, something else happened: I hardly talked to the people at the factory back home. In fact, I don't think I talked to them more than once or twice all that week. I was stunned to discover that they could continue operating without my constant presence! It was true—they really could run the place without me, regardless of what I thought. And that was when I decided not to accept the new promotion. It was basically a title with a very small increase in salary but a massive increase in pressure and responsibility. No, thank you, sir.

I took Amy out to dinner one night and shared with her everything I had been thinking. I told her that I wanted to make our family a priority by getting out of my job and that I planned to do so by getting into real estate. When I told her that our path to financial freedom was buying a bunch of rental properties, she thought I was nuts. She said, "But that's just going to take more of your time!"

I reassured her that if I could just buy enough of these rental properties and get them up and running profitably, I could make plenty of money to quit my job and be a full-time husband and dad.

After some encouraging and cajoling, I got Amy to grudgingly go along with my crazy scheme to be the next real estate mini-mogul. The plan to get rich through real estate sounded pretty good on paper, and it sounded almost like winning the lottery if you were to judge by the excited people on the late-night infomercials. But I was about to discover that what you see on TV is not always how things turn out in real life.

REAL ESTATE AND DESPERATION

To map out a course of action and follow it to an end requires some of the same courage that a soldier needs.[42]

—Ralph Waldo Emerson

When we returned to Michigan, my first order of business was to turn down the offer for the promotion. I needed to meet with my boss, Rick Van Vuren, and let him know the bad news. Now, Rick is actually a friend of mine today and was a really positive influence on me while I was working under him. He would frequently take me aside and teach me a lot about people skills and leadership. I owed Rick a lot, and turning down the promotion meant saying no to a friend.

"Rick, I'm honored and flattered you would even consider me for this position," I said when we met in his office, "especially considering I don't yet have my degree in engineering. I'm still in college working towards it. But, Rick, I can't accept this promotion. It's not the road that I want to take."

Rick was stunned. Here was this twenty-nine-year-old kid who had raced up the corporate ladder, getting promotion after promotion, working late all these nights, and now he was saying no! Even worse, Rick had been the one to recommend me to upper management for the promotion. He had vouched for me and really pushed them to let him do this, and now I was torpedoing his plans. He would have some egg on his face if I didn't accept.

"Tim, if you say no to this promotion, that's the end of your career here," he explained. "You'll be severing all of your ties with management. You'll never be considered for another promotion again. You realize that, right?" He shook his head. "I just can't let you turn this down. I can't let you do it."

I said, "Well, Rick, you don't have to 'let' me do it, because I'm going to do it. I'm not taking the job. So you can get rid of me if you want, but the answer is no."

Rick assured me that they wouldn't fire me over this, but he asked me again to really think about my decision. I told him that I had spent a week in Florida with my family and that it was all I had thought about, and my mind was made up—this was what I was doing.

Throughout the next week, Rick tried to convince me to change my mind. My answer never changed. He didn't tell upper management about my decision for about a week; I guess he was hoping I would reconsider. I did feel a little bad for him, personally, because he had been the one to recommend me. What he didn't understand was that I was the stubborn Viking, and my mind was made up. I was out of there; it was just a matter of time.

Now that I had my sights set on real estate, I did the same thing with real estate that I did with Zig Ziglar: I bought every cassette tape and VHS video I could get my hands on. I devoured the information. Most people buy the training programs and never do anything with them. I borrowed $5,000 against my 401(k) and got busy buying homes.

In nine months, I had purchased thirty-three units. I took all the good stuff that Zig taught me about goals and goal-setting and used it to draw up my plan for financial freedom. I used the $5,000 I borrowed to buy the first four or five houses. Once those houses started throwing off some cash, I used the money to get into the next batch of houses. I figured I could keep my job in the daytime to pay our bills while I built up the rental income to a nice level.

Running around managing these houses was starting to eat into my time in a big way. Amy was right! I realized that one person couldn't juggle all of this very well, so I hired a property manager to take care of all the details. It seemed to me that she was doing a decent job of taking care of the properties, but I soon discovered that hiring her was one of the biggest mistakes I had ever made.

Nine months into the deal, I got a letter from one of the real estate programs I had bought. It was a survey form asking how I was doing with building my real estate business. The survey form asked questions like: "How many properties have you bought?" and "What is your net worth?" At the time, I had acquired thirty-three units, and each of the properties was worth between $25,000 and $70,000. That translated into an impressive amount of real estate that I had purchased. (At least, it caught the attention of the people doing the survey.)

I filled out the survey and mailed it back. A few months later, I got a phone call from them. Apparently, I was doing a pretty good job buying up properties, and they thought my story might impress their customers. They called and asked if I would like to be a guest on their next infomercial and tell people about what I had learned from listening to their cassettes.

Well, truth be told, I really hadn't learned that much from their program! I had used so many programs that I just figured out my own system and started working it. I didn't have a system I could learn from, let alone a mentor guiding me. I was finding my own way through the proverbial minefield. And none of the mines had blown up on me . . . *yet*.

I told the lady on the phone as much. "I don't really use your program," I answered. "I won't go on the air and lie. I really just came up with my own way of doing things."

The lady on the phone persisted. "Well, there has to be something you got out of our program, right?"

I thought about it and said, "Well, I suppose it taught me to think outside the box.

And she said, "Great! We'd like to fly you down to Florida on our dime so you can be a part of our new infomercial."

Never one to say no to a free trip to Florida, off to the airport I went. The infomercial crew had *rented* a beautiful home right on the Atlantic Coast. It really looked first class, but it showed off success in a fake way. When I arrived, I met this real estate "guru" for the first time, and from what I could tell, he didn't even do real estate! (Let that be a lesson, in case you ever decide to buy stuff from a late-night infomercial: Make sure the person isn't some charlatan who is talking a lot of hot air. Rather, seek out information from people who have successfully done what you want to do.)

Anyway, I found myself sitting in this room with all these other guests who were going to appear on the show. And I went around the room asking everyone if they used this guy's real estate course to get rich. And everyone had the same answer I did! No one used the course, and we were all about to be his promotional guests on his infomercial! That just proves that not everything you see on TV is true!

After the infomercial, the reality of running my real estate "empire" was sinking in. It really was a self-employed S-quadrant business, like Robert Kiyosaki talks about in his book *Cashflow Quadrant*.[43] I was running ragged from one house to the next, fixing leaky toilets, collecting rent here, and managing an issue there. The property manager I hired *seemed* to be doing a good job keeping the places rented and managing the repair bills. But instead of giving me my freedom, the real estate business proved to be another huge yoke on my shoulders.

Amy's prediction during our Florida trip was coming true: This was just one more thing that was keeping me busy and away from our family. And now that I was really making my family time a priority (or trying to, as best I could), I soon came to the conclusion that my real estate plan was not working out the way I had hoped it would. I knew I wanted to be financially free. I knew I needed to do something. I knew that somehow, there just had to be a better way.

THE BUSINESS OF LEADERSHIP

One of the most difficult things everyone has to learn is that for your entire life, you must keep fighting and adjusting if you hope to survive. No matter who you are or what your position is, you must keep fighting for whatever it is you desire to achieve.[44]

—George Allen

Between working at the automotive supply company and running my real estate business, I was exposed to some colorful characters. One day at work, I got introduced to a coworker named Bill Lewis. Now, Bill made quite an entrance back then. The first time I ever saw him, he was dressed in a red Adidas silk track suit, and he had just arrived at work. Maybe he was coming from the gym, but my first thought was, "This guy is wearing his pajamas to work!" On top of that, he was wearing some nice gold chains around his neck. I saw them and chuckled to myself, "Wow! A genuine Mr. T Starter Kit!" Bill was a pretty fashionable guy back then!

I sort of judged Bill negatively and wrote him off at first. But then I got to chatting with him and discovered we had some common interests—namely, real estate. Bill also was getting involved in rental properties and even owned a few at the time. I thought, "Hey, this is my kind of guy!" And that opened the door to my liking and respecting him. Bill checked out my properties, and I checked out some of his. We looked at some deals together, although we never ended up doing any. Well, it turned out that Bill and his other buddy at work had gotten themselves into some sort of leadership business. At the time, it just sounded to me like a cheesy get-rich-quick scheme, or so my closed-minded Viking personality thought. When they tried to approach me about it, I brushed them both off. After a while, their persistence—actually, back then it seemed like pestering to grumpy old Tim—started to wear me down.

I finally said to Bill, "If I sign up in this deal with you, will you leave me alone?"

He assured me he would. I signed up, handed him a check, and that was the end of it – or so I thought.

You see, while this was happening, my real estate business was starting to crumble. I was scrambling around trying to keep afloat, and every week, there were Bill and our colleague, smiling and cheerful, saying fun things to bug me, like, "Fired up!" Frankly, I wasn't feeling too fired up about my life, so their cheerfulness rubbed me the wrong way. There they were at the office, always excited about their Tuesday-night association meeting. Week after week, they would invite me to this meeting to learn how to make money, and every Tuesday, I would make up an excuse not to go. This went on for four months. They kept talking about these two guys Chris Brady and Orrin Woodward. I almost went to their business meeting just to see what an "Orrin" was!

And then I hit rock bottom. My real estate venture had imploded. I discovered that the team I trusted to run my business had been doing some things behind my back that basically put me out of business. I thought I had built a $1.3 million empire with thirty-three rental properties, but I discovered that many of them were vacant, and I was facing foreclosure with a lot of my portfolio. All of a sudden, I was $1.3 million in debt. I couldn't even make a payment on my own home. I was about to lose everything, and I didn't know how to face my family and tell them I had totally screwed up.

I remember coming home late at night, and Cam was asleep on the couch. He had tried to wait up for me, but he had grown too tired. I was just broken; I touched his soft little face and wept quietly. "I'm so sorry, little buddy," I said, all choked up. "Daddy messed up." I picked him up and put him in his bed, and I lay down in my own bed for yet another sleepless night.

I ended up at a church one Tuesday, and I just prayed for hours. I would get up to leave and then collapse back down on my knees. I prayed and prayed to God to give me an answer – any sign of hope, any way out, any possible opportunity to dig myself out of the financial mess I was in. I walked out of the church, and I remembered that it was Tuesday night. I grumbled aloud, "Oh great, I promised Bill Lewis that I would go to that stupid business meeting tonight."

At that moment, it was as though the clouds had parted and the heavens shone a light down upon me! I imagined little angels flying all around and choir voices singing! God had answered my prayers; he had sent me Bill Lewis and the Tuesday meeting! I raced home and grabbed Amy. We got dressed, and out the door we went.

The business meeting that night was one of the greatest turning points in my life. I saw why I was in the mess I was in, as well as a way that I could dig myself out of it. I wasn't even thinking about getting rich; I was in pure survival mode at the time. So we got rocking and rolling.

To say that the next thirty-one months were a blur would be an understatement. I started working hard sharing a vision of creating financial freedom through a leadership business, and I shared it with as many people as I could. I ran as if my life depended on it because it felt as though it did. I was being crushed from all directions and was on the verge of losing everything. If we lost the house, we would be moving in with my in-laws. I loved Amy's parents, but I had zero interest in living in their basement.

Through all of the misadventures, all of the upsets and growth that I had to go through, I had a very special advantage: I had met two wealthy and successful men who had their family values in place and wanted to make a difference in people's lives – two guys who would go on to write a *New York Times* best-selling book on leadership and become the current-ranked seventh and twelfth leadership gurus on the planet. They would befriend me, guide me through some of my darkest hours of need, and see me cross the seven-figure finish line only two and a half years later. They were Chris Brady and Orrin Woodward. And I thank God every day for their presence in my life. Both have greatly helped me, and today Orrin is my mentor and still spends hundreds of hours on me.

When It's Too Hard to Stand, Fall to Your Knees

This was the time in my life when I grew more spiritually than ever before. I knew the Lord before then, but I believe that right in the middle of all of my financial struggles was when God really accelerated my sanctification process. It was when I faced the hardest circumstances that I drew closest to God. There is a great saying that goes, "When life gets too hard to stand, fall to your knees." I spent way more time on my knees during those days than I did trying to walk around on my own.

When we use our wisdom alone to guide us, we run into problem after problem, corner after corner. As my business partners like to say, "If you don't like the results you are getting in life, stop taking advice from yourself." During this time, I stopped listening to Tim Marks's wisdom, and I started listening to God and the godly men who were where I wanted to be in life – simple but profound.

> *If you don't like the results you are getting in life, stop taking advice from yourself.*

A lot of people try to have faith in themselves when they should be trying to have faith in God. We should seek His plan in our lives rather than try to make our own way. God won't use you until you are finished with yourself. And I had reached the point where there was nothing more that Tim Marks could do other than try his hardest and have the faith that God would open the next door in front of him.

That's how God works! I had tried everything I could think to do.

When it got to the point where I couldn't even buy groceries for my kids, I wanted to borrow money from people. Once I met him, I even wanted Orrin to loan me some money! I thought, "Man, this guy is so rich, why doesn't he just loan me $20,000 or something, just to get me through the week?" But he never did offer me money, and I was too proud to ask him.

Looking back on it, I'm glad Orrin never wavered. I have struggled with wanting to loan people money because when you lead an organization the size of mine, it's only a matter of time before you see some people who are in dire financial circumstances. I've actually called Orrin, asking him if he thought it was okay for me to loan money to some people on my business team who were hurting. I'd say, "Orrin, this guy is in a real jam. He can pay me back in three weeks!"

And Orrin would stop me and ask, "Tim, how much money did I ever loan you?"

And I would answer, "Not a penny."

"Tim," he said, "I gave you something far more valuable than money. I gave you the self-respect that you could dig yourself out of the situation you were in."

And I am really thankful to Orrin for that lesson; he never did give me money. Now, please understand: I am *not* saying that you should never loan someone money. What I am saying is that sometimes when we loan money, especially if we loan it to the wrong people, it ends up hurting them. Charity with the people we know has its place, but I feel that it is used too often.

Don't Read Your Press Clippings

My business partners and I have encountered a problem that is so common we have actually given it a name: reading your press clippings. What that describes is someone finally starting to have success and mistakenly deciding to

85

bask in the glory of all the nice things people are saying about them. It's like a sports figure or a celebrity who gets a lot of press in the newspaper sitting around reading that stuff to make him or herself feel important. Sadly, when people's heads get inflated, it usually results in some bad news coming their way.

When I launched my leadership business, I was in such dire financial straits that I had no choice but to run like the wind. Because of that, I probably surprised a lot of people with how fast I started to experience some healthy results. People got to talking about my efforts and started sending a lot of praise my way. And like every other mortal man, I fell victim to a big ego, and I started to read my press clippings.

I started to puff my chest out and fluff up my proverbial peacock feathers a little too much. I started feeling less concerned about my crushing $1.3 million of real estate debt and $15,000 of monthly payments. I started thinking, "Hey, it will take care of itself because I am so good at building leadership communities!" Well, God dealt with my arrogance very quickly.

When my ego went up, my business growth went down. You could almost chart it on a graph. Once I got my ego back in check, things started growing again. After a while, I started to realize that even if I did all the right things, God would not bless me unless I remained humble.

> *DRYPC GIDI: Don't Read Your Press Clippings; God Is Doing It.*

I learned the hard way to be very conscious of who was doing what (God or me). In fact, to remind myself of this truth, I put an acrostic on my steering wheel: DRYPC GIDI. People would see this "code" and wonder what it meant. I would tell them it meant, "Don't Read Your Press Clippings; God Is Doing It." I would look at that every single day and often read it out loud. And as my humility increased, so did my success. I learned through experience that

> *I learned through experience that humility is one of the main ingredients to reaching our goals.*

humility is one of the main ingredients in reaching goals.

Expand Your Vision of What's Possible

One of my favorite books is *The Magic of Thinking Big*.[45] I regularly recommend it to people as they begin their own journey to success, and I like to follow up on their progress and ask them what they have learned from the book. Sometimes I'll get someone saying, "Well, Tim, I've learned that I just need to think bigger!" Hey, at least they read the cover!

We each need to expand our vision of what is possible, even in really terrible times. In fact, it's even more important to think big when our outlook is grim. That's when we need the most hope and faith for a brighter future.

When Amy and I were struggling financially, we used to have really small goals. For example, when we were living in our first house, we had this huge dream of renovating the deck out back. We dreamed of how neat it would be to put up storm windows and add some flooring and make it a nice room that we could use.

A contractor had come up with a quote on the work; he figured it would take $3,800 to do the job. I was sunk. At the time, $3,800 might as well have been $38 million. I couldn't fathom how anyone could have that amount of extra money just lying around to put into storm windows and remodeling. I thought, "Someday, Tim, someday . . . you'll be rich enough to be able to afford storm windows." Boy, was I thinking small!

After Orrin Woodward had started mentoring me, he helped straighten out my thinking and expand my vision. He finally got me to stop thinking about those $3,800 windows and to start thinking about something bigger! He said, "Don't try to patch up your current situation—try to change your situation! Get the heck out of there!"

Orrin was absolutely right. I had built so many negative memories of defeat in that house that it would always be a reminder of those bad feelings. I needed to move on.

In time, we moved into our new home, and then to another one after that. We had achieved a little more financial success. And do you know what? After a while, I totally forgot about my original goal until one day after I had bought our "little shack" by the ocean and a bunch of toys and had helped many friends become financially free, I was going down memory lane and got to thinking about that dingy old starter home. And I recalled that I had missed my *original* goal. In the midst of all of the hoopla, I had completely forgotten about the original goal of getting storm windows!

Most of the time, a lot of us get concerned with accomplishing itty-bitty goals, rather than taking a big bite out of life and going after some big, hairy, audacious goals (as Jim Collins likes to say in his excellent book *Good to Great*[46]). When we don't think big enough with our goals, it's probably because we don't think big enough of ourselves. We have to see the good in ourselves and our infinite potential. When we choose to think big, it's the one and only thing that is going to propel us forward.

> *When we don't think big enough with our goals, it's probably because we don't think big enough of ourselves.*

So we need to stop thinking small! Instead of thinking, "I need to put new tires on my old car, or I need a new paint job for my old car," we should be thinking, "Let's go buy a new car! Let's buy a new one that doesn't need a paint job. We don't have to paint our yucky ugly old car. We must get another car that doesn't need one!" Think *big*.

Finally, Things Were Starting to Happen

I remember sitting at my kitchen table and thinking for the first time, "We're going to make it." When I opened the mail, I calculated that our income that month from my leadership business, after expenses, was going to be $35,000. I had never in my life made that much money in a single month. I said out loud, "Wow. We're one of 'them' — those people who have 'made it.'" Honestly, it was a little surreal.

Now, Amy and I weren't out of the financial woods yet. We still had $800,000 in debt to pay off at that point, so while my $35,000 was great, it was only going to put a dent in the problem. We were going backwards $15,000 a month, so $35,000 was nice, but we certainly weren't going shopping for fun with that money. Orrin was counseling me to pay off all of my mortgages and loans very aggressively.

I would go to a closing of one of my houses, and sometimes I would pocket $2,000. Some closings would cost me $30,000 just to walk away from the property. That $35,000 check just showed me that the cash flow was there. What was new was that I could see the light at the end of the tunnel. It gave me hope that we were going to make it. I could physically feel at least some of the weight coming off my shoulders.

Once God had humbled me, I realized I hadn't caused my success; all the credit went to the Lord. When we hit our first $100,000 month, I finally felt that I wasn't really pressed for money. I was making enough cash so I could afford to buy a Corvette every month of the year. I also realized that I didn't need to show off the cash; it was far more rewarding to help people than to buy a lot of toys.

Our financial situation improved rapidly over a period of thirty-one months. The thought of how fast things turned around and went from really bad to really good almost makes my head spin. We had been living in a $200,000 house, and we had been so broke that we almost lost it. We paid that house off completely and moved into a new home. That particular house was 2,800 square feet on the water on a canal on the Gulf of Mexico. When we bought it, we put down a big hunk in cash. Then we paid the remainder off in sixteen months.

Let's just say that my financial picture is different today than it used to be. My life has turned around in every way, and if Tim Marks, the Viking, can do it with all of his rough edges, I know that you can do it, too. I know that many people doubt themselves and their ability to win in life, but perhaps if you know I was able to dig myself out of the financial hole I was in, then you might be inspired to feel that you could do so as well.

I don't feel any need to brag or cast light on myself. I certainly don't want anyone being impressed with me for having some fancy toys; really, it's not my desire for anyone to be impressed with me for *any* reason. I could lose all these toys (except maybe the fishing boat - just kidding!) and be just as happy as I am today. In the end, there is only one person I'm trying to impress, and He doesn't care about my toys, considering He allowed me to have them.

The reason I share this laundry list of toys is to expand your vision of what is possible. To get a Mercedes, I had to help hundreds of people. To get a motor coach, I had to help thousands of people. To pay off our debt and purchase our "little shack," I had to help tens of thousands of people. The toys are fun, but they just represent the number of people we've helped along the way.

The biggest victory is not the stuff — it's the relationships that have taken off because of all the personal growth I went through. I got to keep my marriage to the most amazing girl I've ever known. I get to play on the carpet in the middle of the day with my kids and throw the football around in the afternoon with Cam. To think that I went from seven figures in debt to seven figures a year in income is a little too mind-boggling to consider!

It's amazing what you can turn around in thirty-one months if you decide to focus, run on total belief and zero doubt, and listen to the advice of the godly men who have walked the minefield before you. It's a heck of a change from sitting in my dusty basement crying, unable to pay my credit cards or buy food for my kids, to being totally out of debt and earning over $100,000 a month only two and a half years later.

Ironically, no matter how far we have come, there will always be funny reminders of where we came from to make us smile and keep us humble. Despite having gained a little respect in the leadership industry, I still earned a few chuckles one night. We were out at a restaurant eating wings with some associates, celebrating a great quarter of growth. Like many restaurants these days, there was a whole bank of television monitors that were on behind me so everybody could watch the ballgame.

My business associates started staring at the screens, and they even began to point and laugh out loud! Finally, I couldn't stand not knowing what was going on. I said, "What? What?" I turned around to see what they were looking at. Well, there on the monitors behind me was Mr. Baldy himself—Tim Marks in all his glory – on television with the Florida infomercial, smiling for the camera as the "guru" pitched the benefits of purchasing some no-money-down real estate.

Some people just have bad college photos buried in a yearbook to remind them of their goofy mistakes. Me? No, sir, when I do something silly, I like to do it *big*.

CONCLUSION

L ike many people, I wanted to be on the fast track to success in life, but I made the mistake of not determining first the correct track on which I should be. I was never taught "define, learn, do." I had to come to this truth through a lot of painful trial-and-error. It wasn't enough to just get promotions at work; I eventually realized that true success meant having a fulfilling marriage, beating my addiction to alcohol, and being a great dad to Cameron. It also meant finding my salvation through my Lord and Savior Jesus Christ. I would not have been able to endure the crushing setbacks and financial disaster brought about by my adventures in real estate had I not had a strong faith in my Lord. When true opportunity for financial abundance came, I learned to remain humble and give thanks to Him for the blessings in my life.

KEY POINTS

1. The formula for success is simple: Define what you want, learn what is needed to accomplish the goal, and then do

what is required to achieve it.

2. Addictions don't begin obviously; instead, they slip in quietly when we let our guards down and we are weak.

3. Don't fool yourself into thinking you are not an addict – whether it is an addiction to alcohol, drugs, or pornography. You can't get better unless you admit you have a problem. Reach out to someone you trust and say, "I think I may have a problem, and I'm just looking to talk."

4. Tragedy tends to wake us up to what's really important in our lives. I didn't realize how precious my mom really was to me until her health started to fail.

5. If you think you are successful at work but a failure in your marriage, your health, and your spiritual life, don't be so quick to consider yourself a success.

6. DRYPC DIDI. Don't Read Your Press Clippings; God Is Doing It. Remember Ephesians 2:8–9: "For it is by grace you have been saved through faith. And this is not your own doing; it is the gift of God, not a result of works, so that no one may boast"(ESV). Remain humble.

7. When life gets too hard to stand, fall to your knees.

8. We don't think big enough with our goals because we don't think big enough of ourselves. Don't set itty-bitty goals. Set *big* goals.

THE CHARACTER OF A VIKING

A constant struggle, a ceaseless battle to bring success from inhospitable surroundings, is the price for all great achievements.[47]

—Orison Swett Marden

Whenever people say the word *Viking*, most of us tend to get a picture in our heads of ancient warriors from a faraway land: men who would arrive in their boats to raid, pillage, and burn a town to the ground before racing off with their loot. The movies we watch show us pictures of guys wearing helmets with big horns, worshiping their pagan gods like Thor and Odin, and smashing their enemies with an axe or a sword in one hand while carrying a big turkey drumstick in the other. Well, after a little reading and research, I discovered that there sure was a lot of raiding and pillaging going on! Those stories had a lot of truth to them. But it was also interesting to find that it wasn't the *whole* story.

I thought I should share with you some of the things that I've learned about Vikings: the good, the bad, and the ugly. In confronting brutal reality, I had to take an honest look at myself and realize that all the things I was doing to earn the nickname the Viking were probably not helping me in the long run. I was tough on people. But I also worked hard and got a lot accomplished. I think it would be fair to say that being the Viking was a double-edged sword, and I needed help figuring out which side of the blade to use (or better yet, how to cover one side of the blade with velvet).

> *I think it would be fair to say that being the Viking was a double-edged sword, and I needed help figuring out which side of the blade to use (or better yet, how to cover one side of the blade with velvet).*

It became an interesting endeavor to dig into some Viking history to see if I could discover some lessons to help me make sense of my being that way. The more I learned about the Vikings, the more I realized that this community had a lot of powerful qualities that we can learn from, especially today.

A LITTLE VIKING HISTORY: THE GOOD, THE BAD, AND THE UGLY

The Vikings definitely earned their name. They did a lot of terrible things—things that we would be horrified to even think about in today's world. In fact, the word *Viking* actually means "one who fights at sea—a pirate or a robber" and "warfare at sea or harrying"[48] (not a great name for someone to earn back then or to have as a nickname today). But to be fair, any invading warrior of those times did the same terrible things.

A big part of the reason we have this picture of the Vikings as being violent and brutal raiders is that a lot of recorded history came from the Christian churches of the day. For quite some time, the Vikings had a nasty habit of attacking Christian settlements (especially before they converted to Christianity). So when you're the Christian missionary writing notes about the pagan warriors from another country who arrived to carry off your women and slaughter your men, *your* version of history tends to reflect that you're feeling pretty ticked off about how the day went![49]

The other thing to remember is that even today, peaceful activities don't make the news; it's the really bad stuff that does. I guess it just wasn't as interesting for the reporters even back then to write about peaceful, positive encounters. So for every violent raid that was talked about and recorded for all of history, there were plenty of peaceful trade missions with the Vikings that were ignored.

The history of Denmark, Sweden, and Norway describes the Vikings as courageous warriors; while history everywhere else in Europe describes the Vikings as violent thugs. (Imagine if they had had Internet blogs back then: The Vikings could have sneezed the wrong way, and it would have

> It's a good point to remember that as you are searching for the facts, you have to keep in mind whose side of the story you are hearing.

been all over the Internet that they burned a town to the ground.) It's a good point to remember that as you are searching for the facts, you have to keep in mind whose side of the story you are hearing.

Else Roesdahl, author of *The Vikings*, says that the picture we have of Vikings isn't really complete:

It used to be thought that Vikings were just energetic, robust, straightforward people or that they were wild, axe-wielding pirates; and that they lived in a fairly democratic society. The Viking Age is now seen as having been altogether more complex, with a strong class system, diverse social conditions and far more radical achievements. In an era of rapid change, the Vikings took every advantage of their unusual ability to readjust, and their gift for enterprise produced quite exceptional results and innovations."[50]

The ancient people of Denmark, Sweden, and Norway did a lot more than I had realized: They built really active trading towns, they traded goods with other countries, they negotiated peace treaties with different kings, and they mastered a lot of complicated engineering such as building bridges and fortresses. I was a little relieved that these guys weren't *all* bad!

The Vikings Yearned for Freedom

Since the beginning, people everywhere have wanted to be free. It's a hunger that lives in every person—the idea that you can call your own shots, that you don't have to live under anyone else's thumb, and that you can make your life as great as you want it to be. People from every time in history and every country seem to be born with this desire, and the Vikings were no different. In fact, freedom was a major part of Viking society.

The Viking society was made up of three classes of people: the rich, the common free men, and the slaves. Many Vikings were free men, and you could think of them as today's middle-class. They made up the "realm's backbone."[51] What is interesting to me is that the vast majority of free people were self-employed business owners: They owned and ran farms, they hunted for food for the community, they were blacksmiths and silversmiths, they traded goods and services, they were mercenaries for hire, and they rented land to other people. Else Roesdahl says, "In practice, the concept of freedom may have depended on a certain amount of wealth."[52] That is still true today.

Free people had a lot of privileges. They got to voice their opinions publicly in a type of town-hall meeting called the "Thing." They got to vote, could carry an axe or sword to protect themselves, and had legal protection in the community under the laws of the land.

It was great to be free! (Or at least, it was definitely better than being a slave.) Slaves, on the other hand, did not have a very pleasant daily life. In fact, it was a custom in the days of the Vikings that if the master died, the slave was tossed into the grave and either beheaded or buried alive along with him.[53] (And you think getting laid off *today* is bad. Back then, if the *boss* went, *you* went, too!)

I see a lot of similarities today. A lot of people today are free because they choose to own a small business and take control of their own destinies. It takes a lot of guts to do so, and I applaud anyone with the courage to step out on his or her own. Most people want a safe, secure job with a boss who calls the shots. Just like in the days of the Vikings, it

> *The way to freedom is the same today as it was a thousand years ago.*

leaves people trapped under the boss's thumb. But when people realize that the way out of bondage is to own land, to own a farm, to own a shop that sells goods, to trade and do business with other men across the village or across the ocean, they are reminded that the way to freedom is the same today as it was a thousand years ago.

The Vikings Were Courageous Explorers

No matter what your opinion of the Vikings might be, the one thing you have to be impressed by is the fact that they did not sit around waiting for a handout. The Viking culture existed from AD 780 to AD 1070.[54] This was a pretty rough time to grow up and raise a family, let alone build a village, in any country. Land didn't always produce crops, the weather wasn't nearly as nice as it is here in Florida, babies didn't always survive childbirth, and getting a cold sometimes meant you were toast.

So imagine you are a dad, your family is starving, the crops didn't grow the way you hoped, and you are about to freeze to death. What do you do? A Viking wasn't about to sit around and watch his wife and kids die. So he picked up a sword, hopped on a boat, and went looking for a means to help his family survive. And with no moral compass to guide him at that time, let alone a Bible, it usually meant becoming a raider.

In fact, once the Vikings realized they could make a lot more money (and capture slaves) by being raiders, it became one of the more popular careers among them. Like people today, they wanted to provide for their families, create wealth, and have good lives. They quickly figured out that they had the engineering abilities to make boats and weapons that would let them steal what they wanted from neighboring villages and countries. Soon it became a way of life for a whole segment of the population.[55]

Their ambition produced boats, and the men aboard those boats set sail for new lands. And did they ever discover new lands! The Vikings were responsible for colonizing Iceland and Greenland, and they settled in parts of England and Russia. In fact, despite the common belief that Christopher Columbus was the first to arrive in America, the truth is that the Vikings actually beat him to the punch by about five hundred years, having discovered America around AD 1000. They had figured out how to navigate the waters and make their way back home by the stars. They were true adventurers seeking to return home with the loot so that their families would prosper.[56]

I can imagine that sailing the seas back then was not the most enjoyable trip. It was not like traveling on a Carnival Cruise liner today. Men would get sick and die on the way, they would be injured and have no medical help at all, and they were probably worried about being eaten by sea monsters or falling off the edge of the earth. Those boats of theirs weren't the seagoing battleships of America today; they were handcrafted with tools that were made by hand as well. Imagine going into a forest, chopping down some trees to build a boat, and then sailing across the Atlantic. That's what those guys did. Please understand, I don't condone or make any apologies for their very ungodly raiding and pillaging—it was awful. But I do believe that exploring new lands takes a lot of guts and a lot of faith that things will be all right.

It can be scary to face the unknown. Every explorer has faced that. You will face some fears when you attempt a big adventure of your own. Sometimes we have to get on the boat and start paddling for new lands because it's what our family needs us to do, even if it seems scary. Even if we think that they want us to stay on the

> *One does not discover new lands without consenting to lose sight of the shore for a very long time.*
> *— Andre Gide*

dock and be safe, our responsibility as a leader is to lead. Sometimes we have to risk everything in order to get the big victory. One thing I know for sure, as Andre Gide says: "One does not discover new lands without consenting to lose sight of the shore for a very long time."[57]

The Vikings Connected Communities

A lot of us today use a technology called Bluetooth to allow our cell phones and wireless devices to connect. When I first heard the name of the technology, I thought it seemed a little strange. But it turns out that there is a bit of interesting Viking history attached to it. The Bluetooth technology is literally named after a Viking king, Harald "Bluetooth" Gormsson, king of Denmark in AD 958. (The symbol for the Bluetooth is actually his first and last initials combined.)

So why would anyone choose a name like *Bluetooth* to describe technology that unites different devices and gets people to communicate? The name is appropriate because Harald "Bluetooth" Gormsson is famous in Denmark for having united the people into one great kingdom.[58] He also united the religious beliefs of his land by bringing Christianity to the pagan people of Denmark. As the story goes, Bluetooth had been visited by a Christian missionary, whom he challenged to prove that his Christian God could perform miracles. The missionary held a white-hot poker to his hand and showed Bluetooth that his hand had not been burned. Well, that was a good-enough demonstration for Bluetooth! He was pretty much sold on Christianity at that point and decided that all of Denmark ought to become Christian along with him.[59]

Part of the process of uniting his kingdom was another important activity: building bridges. In fact, for the Vikings, "grand bridge-building was also considered an honorable and Christian deed."[60] During his time as king, Bluetooth made a point of building bridges — big ones, and lots of them. It's pretty obvious that this would be helpful for practical reasons, such as for allowing soldiers to go where they needed to be, townsfolk to move their crops to the market, and merchants to travel to other towns to sell their products.

But philosophically, building a bridge means making a connection with another person, or a group of people. It means being willing to invest time, money, and energy to reach people you wouldn't normally be able to reach. Building a bridge is one of the most amazing ways of saying, "I value you, and I value our connection."

> *Building a bridge is one of the most amazing ways of saying, "I value you, and I value our connection."*

In our lives, we also want to build bridges to reach the people we care about. But the bridges I mean may not be physical. Building a bridge might mean that we pick up the phone to reach out to someone who has gone through a tough time, or someone who needs some guidance. It might mean staying behind an extra ten minutes at a business meeting to encourage a new colleague. It might mean leaving work early to coach your son's soccer team. It definitely means creating a stronger connection with people. I think we can learn a lesson from history here and set a goal for ourselves to become better connectors and better bridge-builders in each area of our lives.

WHEN YOU'RE A HAMMER, EVERYTHING LOOKS LIKE A NAIL

Love blinds us to faults, but hatred blinds us to virtues.[61]

—Iba Ezra

Vikings are not exactly the most gentle people around. They are a pretty tough lot. You might say that a true Viking warrior has a choleric, or a type D, personality. He is the general of his own little army. The military calls it a type A personality. Whatever you call it, if you have a fly on your forehead, a Viking will want to kill it — with an axe.

The Vikings sure get things done, but they can leave a trail of bodies in their wake. Sometimes, they get blamed for not being "touchy-feely" enough. That's not really true. When a Viking "touches" you with his proverbial hammer, you're going to "feel" it!

Sometimes we might accuse the Vikings of not caring enough about people. A true Viking cares about people. Unfortunately, it is usually in the form of how many people he has beaten, or how many people are lined up on his side, ready to fight the enemy. If you are going to help a Viking get results and win the battle, a true Viking warrior probably thinks you are just great. But if you are sitting on the sidelines watching the fight, a Viking might ignore you.

I earned the nickname the Viking because of my bad attitude and my bad treatment of people. At my old job with the leading automotive manufacturing company, I had developed quite a reputation for my people skills. To be clear, the reputation was that I didn't have *any* people skills.

I remember one time when I was walking up to the office door of Bernie, my boss's boss. He and another guy were talking and laughing, and something made me think that they were talking about me. I asked them, "What's up?"

Bernie said, "John here was looking for you, and I just told him that if he ever needed to find Tim Marks, he should just go out into the factory and look for the trail of blood and body parts."

Bernie didn't even normally work at our plant, but my reputation was so bad it had gone all the way up the corporate ladder to the guys outside the building. I was not the type of guy whom you would ever expect to lead people in a business. I sure knew how to bully people and threaten them that they would get fired if they didn't do what I said. I also knew how to yell at people and make them feel terrible. But sarcasm was my weapon of choice, and even today, I still have to fight the urge to use it.

I was the ultimate "positional leader." People followed me only because the company organizational chart said they had to. If I didn't have their paychecks to hold over their heads, they wouldn't have listened to a thing I barked at them to do. I wasn't a leader—I was a manager-slash-dictator. I had plenty of power but zero influence. If I had been leading a volunteer army, I would have found myself walking alone because no one would have tolerated my abusive behavior.

I knew I had to change in order to grow into the leader that I wanted to be. I knew I had to soften my heart to people and love them where they were. I also knew that in order to be able to soften my heart to people, I would have to change the way I thought. I realized that

> *I knew I had to change in order to grow into the leader that I wanted to be.*

changing myself would be one of the hardest things I would ever do. But the price of failure was way too big, and the reward for changing was way too exciting.

Why Use an Axe When You Can Use Sarcasm?

A sarcastic person has a superiority complex that can be cured only by the honesty of humility.[62]

—Lawrence G. Lovasik

Some people might assume that a Viking would always be overly aggressive—yelling and chewing people out. I never really did that; even today, it is difficult for me to get angry and yell at people, which is something that God has blessed me with. However, I have been cursed with sarcasm, and for a long time, that was my weapon of choice.

Even today, after all these years of hard work on grinding away my bad people skills, I still have to be on guard against using sarcasm. Some people might be really crafty with their words and not offend people. I am not one of them. I could never dream of getting away with saying some of the things I hear other leaders say. They make it funny; I would say the same statement, and it would come out hurtful. I've learned it's best to err on the side of caution today and avoid sarcasm. (If you must use it, I'd suggest that you use it only on yourself.) However, I didn't always avoid it. No, sometimes I used to really enjoy being sarcastic and cutting people down.

I remember one time when I was called into the plant at the automotive manufacturing company, and I was not happy about being up in the middle of the night. A robot had broken down, and it was the responsibility of my team to get it up and running. Now, we had invested thousands of dollars in training these guys how to maintain the robots, so I was expecting them to be on the ball. By the time I arrived at the plant in the middle of the night, I was in a right foul mood. And it was never good if the problem took me only ten seconds to fix.

I got to the plant and saw that it was a case of a safety switch that needed to be flipped. One button, and the robot was up and running. I looked at the robot programmer, really disgusted that I had to be dragged down there at three o'clock in the morning, and I said something gentle and forgiving like, "So do we need to send you to another $5,000 class, or are you all set now? Do you understand how to manage this?"

I can remember the look of shock and hurt in the programmer's face. I thought he was being melodramatic, and I didn't even bother to consider how he felt. But if I was being bothered and awakened at three o'clock in the morning, I figured that justified my tearing him down to make him look horrible and to make me look good. And that was my honest goal a lot of the time, I'm ashamed to say.

My goal was to tear people down so they knew I was better than they were. This made me feel superior. I remember a time when a forklift driver was trying to get something off of the rack. He was struggling with it, and I was getting impatient. I kicked him off and jumped in, saying, "Get out of the way, I'll get that thing down." I got the stuff off of the rack and set it down on the ground.

I couldn't leave well enough alone. I had to end this with a little verbal jab to make the forklift driver feel bad. I said in a really condescending way, "There you go, buddy. That's how you do it. If you need any other help doing your job, just let me know. After all, that's only the second time I've driven a forklift."

Not only was I being hurtful, I was embellishing the truth. I had driven the forklift many times by then in order to know how to do the job right, but I wanted to make myself look better than I was.

I had no patience or grace with people. I totally ignored the fact that people needed time to learn their jobs and that even the best of us have bad days where we don't perform at 100 percent. It pains me today to think of how I treated people. I gave no thought to how they were doing. How could I know if they were going through a divorce, or that they had a sick family member? I just didn't care what the excuse was.

I wish I had been gracious and thoughtful. It is so easy to simply say, "Hey, you look like you're having a tough day; do you need some help?" Or I could have just said, "Is there something I can do to help?" That would have been a much better way of approaching the situation. With the forklift driver, I could have stood back and offered some suggestions, rather than shoving him aside and taking over. He would have learned and improved, but because I was his boss, I thought I didn't have to be kind and that I could just push him around.

We Are Blind to Our Blind Spots

The greatest obstacle to discovery is not ignorance—it is the illusion of knowledge.[63]

—Daniel Boorstin

I honestly couldn't see how much of a jerk I was. Part of the problem of being a Viking or a choleric personality is that one might be totally unaware that he is hurting people. And I was so hurtful to people and was disliked to such a degree that no one wanted to be around me, for any reason.

In the past, I used to ride snowmobiles in Northern Michigan. I had three of them, and thought I'd invite a couple of my guys to go with me one weekend. The first guy I invited said, "Uh, sorry, Tim, I don't have any money."

"No problem!" I said. "I'll pay!" But he wouldn't budge. I offered the same thing to a couple of other guys, but no one wanted to go. This should have been a clue to me, but it wasn't. They couldn't stomach hanging out with me even if it meant getting to have some fun snowmobiling! I was so blind to my bad behavior that it never dawned on me how much they hated me. But the problem with most of us is that unless we are looking for our blind spots, we can't find them and improve.

One time, I was managing a programmer who was a pretty negative guy. Now, despite my rough edges, I really thought of myself as a positive guy, in the sense that I had a can-do attitude. I don't have a lot of patience with people who focus on the obstacles. I have always felt that if there is a job to be done, we should get going and quit the whining!

> But the problem with most of us is that unless we are looking for our blind spots, we can't find them and improve.

Well, I had an issue with something the programmer had done, and I pretty much violated every rule of good people skills: I criticized him – in public *and* in front of his girlfriend. He was so shocked and hurt by this that he said, "You know what? You are a rotten [bleep-bleep-bleep]!"

Sadly, my reaction was not to examine my own behavior but to think about this guy in a negative way. What I should have done was think, "Wow, this guy seems pretty upset with me. I wonder if there is any truth to what he is saying. Even if his delivery wasn't very polished, are there any lessons I can learn here?" But I didn't ask myself those questions. I just wrote the guy off in my head. I said to myself, "Wow, this guy has a rotten attitude! He thinks that I'm the jerk, but really he is the one with the anger management problem!" Wow! How wrong I was! I had a lot of growing up to do, and I still do today.

We Should Follow the Law and Show Grace

Be gentle to all and stern with yourself.[64]

–Saint Teresa of Avila

The Vikings had their own version of a code of honor. A Viking was expected to be loyal to his family, to his chief or king, and to the master of the house if he had an employer. He had to keep his word (except to the enemy he promised not to invade— Vikings wouldn't hold themselves to that very often!), and he had to treat guests well. And if a Viking stabbed someone in the back, literally or otherwise, he could probably expect some sort of reaction that involved an axe being swung in his direction![65]

As they started to follow the teachings of Christ, the Vikings placed a lot of value on honor and character. To quote author Else Roesdahl, "Personal honor was enhanced by praiseworthy qualities: physical courage; skills; magnanimity; generosity (including sharing their turkey legs at the dinner table); eloquence; cleverness; moderation in some matters; self-control; fellowship; the ability to execute unusual deeds; and, in Christian times, good deeds for society such as bridge-building and church-building."[66]

Just like the ancient Vikings, I always felt that I had a pretty clear moral code to follow, a good sense of right and wrong. That was fine, except that rather than focus on what I needed to fix in myself, I would beat people over the head with my moral code and point out where *they* had screwed up.

In fact, at the time of my conversion to Christ, I turned into a Pharisee of sorts. I wanted so badly to be pure that anyone who cursed in my office at the plant would have to put a dollar in the coffee can on my desk. (Proceeds went to charity.) I am embarrassed to share this story, but unfortunately, that's who I was—a brand-new Christian, but without a very good testimony!

One of the biggest lessons I had to learn was to have a balance of law and grace. I needed to learn to stop being so tough on other people and to focus on just being tough on myself. I needed to hold myself accountable and show grace to the folks with whom I lived and worked. This was not an easy journey for me. I had to focus on removing the plank from my own eye and not focus on the speck in someone else's eye.

One example of this was how dogmatic I used to be in sharing my faith with people. I remember being at a business convention and accepting an award for having achieved an

> *One of the biggest lessons I had to learn was to have a balance of law and grace.*

impressive level of success in my industry. I was invited up onstage to speak for a moment, and I chose to blast the audience with my faith. I basically laid out a pretty harsh gospel message and told the audience members that they had better believe a certain way, and that if they didn't, they weren't "real bright"—and that's the gentle paraphrased version. (That particular technique was *not* covered in the Dale Carnegie book *How to Win Friends and Influence People.*)

A whole bunch of people were offended by how dogmatic and brash I was, and I don't blame them one bit. Looking back on it, I'm a little embarrassed to think about how pushy and rude I must have sounded that day. Orrin had to take me aside and explain things to me. He told me that I should consider that I could be hurting people with the way I was speaking. I felt that I was right, but perhaps my approach could be improved. Over time, I've changed the way I speak on the subject. I still want to challenge people's beliefs, but instead of ramming my opinion down their throats, I like to simply say, "Know why you believe what you believe." This approach is much less confrontational, and it keeps the lines of communication open. If you raise someone's blood pressure, you lose them.

> *If you raise someone's blood pressure, you lose them.*

Orrin Woodward's mentoring, along with my own faith, taught me to soften up my approach with people. I learned that I was commanded to love, and since I have a desire to be obedient, I forced myself to sand off some of my rough edges. (In my case, sanding wasn't enough to get off the rough edges; I had to chisel, grind, and file them away!) This was not a simple task for me. Instead of chewing people out, I had to force myself to bite my tongue.

What I discovered was that if I showed people grace, they would eventually learn the lesson I wanted to teach them through their own leadership learning journey, and my relationship with them would stay intact. Don't get me wrong: There is a time, a place, and a method for offering correction. I just didn't have a clue as to when or what it was. (I've since learned that it's when trust and love exist in the relationship.) But when we are loving toward others and tough on ourselves, it's amazing how relationships can stand the test of time.

> *When we are loving toward others and tough on ourselves, it's amazing how relationships can stand the test of time.*

VIKINGS ARE PROACTIVE

Who hesitate and falter life away, and lose tomorrow the ground won today.[67]

—Matthew Arnold

The Vikings just seemed to get things done. Whether it was building a fort or rowing their boats to faraway lands, these guys were the original go-getters. Some of them were probably a little impulsive; they charged the enemy before they should have. They didn't let fear (or facts!) get in the way; they stepped out and went after what they wanted with courage. And they decided what they wanted to achieve and went after it.

Every moment of every day, we have to decide if we're going to sit on the benches or get onto the playing field. Life doesn't have a pause button that lets us sit around, twiddling our thumbs. Each minute is a magical gift we can never get back. We need to ask, "What am I going to do with this gift? Throw it away or cherish it and make it count?" It takes guts, determination, and energy to keep getting up every time we are knocked down. It takes a really thick skin to keep trucking along when someone we love has cut into our dreams. Some days, it can feel exhausting just to get out of bed. But we need to jump out of bed and get on with the day! Life isn't waiting—it's moving along, with or without our participation. I hope that each of us chooses to squeeze as much life as we can out of every moment we've got.

> *Each minute is a magical gift we can never get back.*

Ready, *Fire*, Aim!

Imperfect action is better than no action.[68]

—Giovanna Garcia

Sometimes, brute strength and bullheaded courage are great qualities. But there is something to be said for pausing and thinking before you act. With my personality, when I'm looking at a task, I like to do things in this pattern: Ready, *fire*, aim. And my results show it. I've gotten a lot done while others were standing around scratching their heads and wondering if they should act. But on the negative side, I've also blown up a lot of things by being a little too fast on the draw.

One example comes to mind. I remember when I walked in on my first day at my new job at the automotive manufacturing plant. I was so excited that I had finally gotten in! Even more impressive was my age: I was in my mid-twenties when I started there. Compared to the rest of the guys working there, I was pretty young. In fact, most of the guys who were working for me were at least ten years my senior, and some were more than that. It would be an understatement to say I was fired up. I was the head of the maintenance department, and I was so pumped up I thought I was going to go in there and change the world!

Well, one of the best examples of my headstrong personality was my lack of a little humility, particularly when it came to admitting what I did and did not know how to do. I was often wrong but never in doubt. One day I found myself alone in front of a big piece of brand-new equipment. Did I know how to use it? Nope. Was I going to wait around and ask for help? Nope! Again, I figured I knew everything about everything. It didn't concern me at all that I had never used this particular piece of equipment and didn't have the first clue as to how to operate it properly.

I sure wasn't going to let the facts get in the way; I just lowered my thick Viking skull and prepared to ram the problem by taking action! (This is a good time to reflect on the fact that if we are humble, we will sure save ourselves a lot of problems later!) Humility is something I have to work on even today, but it was definitely not my strong suit back then.

So the lunch bell rang, and everyone took off to grab a bite to eat. The plant had shut down for an hour, and this left me alone with no one to gently point out the big mistake that I was about to make. I was holding what is called the headliner, or the whole inside of the roof of a car, and I was about to cycle it into the machine. What I didn't realize was that I was supposed to have something called onion skin covering it, which would protect the machine from the material of the headliner. It is kind of like Teflon on a cooking pan.

Well, my arrogance, lack of an onion skin, and the absence of any supervision proved to be a pretty bad combination. The moment I fired up the machine, I knew something was wrong. I could hear grinding and crunching and tearing. The headliner squished together, the steel ground down and popped apart, and the result was a huge sticky mess. All the hydraulics screeched, and the headliner just came apart in the machine. It was just nasty.

The lunch bell rang, and everyone filed back into the plant for work. My staff, the maintenance crew, came back from their break and found their wet-behind-the-ears boss standing in front of this big machine with a huge steaming mess all squished up inside of it. It was pretty ironic that the maintenance manager had personally caused the biggest mess of the day! To say I had egg on my face was a little shy of the truth—I was covered in it!

Well, it took my team hours and hours to get that machine cleaned up. From that day on, it was an uphill battle for me to earn the respect of those guys. Any time they saw me coming near a machine, they would

> *Action is great, but action with a plan and a little humility can be much better!*

say, "Oh no! Look out! Here comes Tim! He's gonna wreck all the machines!" They didn't respect me or trust me all because I lacked the humility to ask for help and figured I was smart enough to do it alone. The moral of the story: Action is great, but action with a plan and a little humility can be much better!

Action Conquers Fear

Panic at the thought of doing a thing is a challenge to do it.[69]
—Henry S. Haskins

I have learned through personal experience and the experience of other leaders that fear can be paralyzing if left unattended. It can hold you back from going after what you want in life. It can cause you to talk yourself out of some of the greatest rewards that life has to offer. And the only antidote to fear is action. Action erases fear. It's like shining a light in a dark basement to scare away the boogeyman, only to discover that there was nothing there. I heard a great saying years ago: "Fear knocked at the front door. Faith answered, and there was no one there." We each might face terrible tragedy and setbacks in our lives—sometimes real, and sometimes exaggerated through our imaginations. When fear tries to discourage us, I believe we should turn to faith for encouragement.

One of the greatest examples of using faith to overcome fear is the story of Bethany Hamilton. I shudder to picture experiencing what she did. Just imagine that you are only thirteen years old, paddling on a surfboard in the waters of Hawaii with your friend and her parents. It's a normal day, October 31, 2003. Suddenly, without warning, you feel something grab your left arm and tug, and you look down to see that your left arm is gone. That's what happened to Bethany Hamilton, a young girl who went through a horrible nightmare and who now uses her story to inspire people.[70]

Bethany was already a surfing champion at her age when the shark attack happened. The shark bit so hard that it bit clean through the surfboard, leaving a dinner-plate-sized chunk missing. It was a miracle that Bethany didn't die from shock on the spot. Bethany looked down and saw that her whole arm was gone. She called out to her friends, "I've been attacked by a shark!" And she started paddling into shore with her remaining arm. They were twenty minutes from the beach. Her friends didn't think she was going to make it.[71]

When they arrived onshore, it seemed as though the whole beach was waiting and an ambulance was on the way. Bethany remembers that as they were loading her into the ambulance, one of the paramedics whispered in her ear, "God will never leave you nor forsake you." They rushed her to the hospital and found that she had lost 40 percent of her blood. She was near death, but the doctors worked around the clock for days to save her, and she survived.[72]

I don't know about you, but I can't imagine going through something like that. It takes a lot of guts and determination just to survive. But what is even more amazing is what Bethany did next. You see, Bethany had always dreamed of surfing. Ever since she was a little kid, she had wanted to be a surfer. The family home movies recorded her surfing when she was just a little girl. Surfing was in her blood, and she loved it. The only problem was that to achieve her dream, she had to go back in the water. So she did something a lot of people would never have the courage to do after such a terrible attack: Bethany Hamilton went back into the water a few months later and started surfing again.[73]

News of her story spread all over the country. She was featured on *The Oprah Winfrey Show*, *The Today Show*, and *Good Morning America*. She became an inspiration for people who have faced terrible situations to have the guts to try again. In fact, her story was featured in a movie called *Soul Surfer*. Bethany credits a lot of the courage required to get back in the water after her accident to her Christian faith, and that faith is an inspiration.[74]

All of us are going to face some Goliaths or some sharks in our lives. A lot of times, those sharks are just in our imagination. For Bethany, it was very real. But she had a choice: Should she give up her dream? Or would she give up her fear? I think she chose the right path. Her decision reminds me of something Frederick W. Cropp said: "There is much in the world to make us afraid. There is much more in our faith to make us unafraid."[75]

Focus on Your Goals and Hit Them

Determine what specific goal you want to achieve. Then dedicate yourself to its attainment with unswerving singleness of purpose, the trenchant zeal of a crusader.[76]

—Paul J. Meyer

Whatever commitments you have made in your life, small or large, focus on those commitments. Focus on the activity you said you were going to do every day. When you do that, it changes who you are and how you look at yourself. Then you can focus on execution and getting results. Chit-chat and good intentions don't pay the bills; results do.

I looked in *Wikipedia* to find the definition of *focus*. What is focus?

Wikipedia has an interesting definition: "Selectively concentrating on one aspect of the environment while other things are going on."[77] Man! If that is not a great definition of focus, I do not know what is. There are so many things that go on day-to-day that we need to do, that it is often difficult to maintain focus on higher commitments.

I love what a very successful psychiatrist Dr. Steve Stokl asks: "What is the single molecule on the tip of your white-hot spear?"[78] What that means to me is: What is the single thing I am focusing on right now? You see, we've only got so much time in the day. There are a lot of good things in life, but only a few great things. There are a lot of ways to make money, but only a few ways to make a difference. I guess I could hire someone to throw the football to my boys or take my daughter on a date, but I'm the best guy for the job. Since we've only got so many days left, we need to think of our time as being very precious. Chris Brady says, "You can't do everything, so choose wisely."

Focus is hard for a lot of people for several reasons. First, life is distracting! Bills have to be paid, food has to be cooked, clothes have to be ironed, and lawns need to be mowed. We get home from work and want to kiss our spouse, play with the kids, and put our feet up with a good book to read. Or for some folks, the game is on TV, and your buddies are coming over. And I haven't even mentioned building volcanoes for the science fair project, driving the girls to dance lessons, or finding time for fishing.

> *Say no to everything good so that you can say yes to everything great.*

So how do you focus? First, we have to decide what our priorities are, and everything else gets put aside. What's the secret to that? It's a simple two-letter word: *no*. As Nancy Reagan used to say, "Just say no!" Say no to all the extra requests and extra projects. Say no to being sucked into little activities, especially when you've got a big mission to accomplish. Say no to everything good so that you can say yes to everything great.

Let me warn you right now: Saying no is one of the hardest things in the world to do because it means denying yourself something that

114

might be fun or rewarding right now. Saying no to another person might also mean that they may not like that. In fact, they might get darn near ornery. (Have you ever noticed that people who have nothing to do want to do it with you?)

> *Have you ever noticed that people who have nothing to do want to do it with you?*

One of the keys to success is that we have to decide what our own goals are. If we don't decide our goals, someone else will. That someone else could be a boss, a family member, or a friend. It could even be our kids! Just because someone else wants us to do something does not automatically mean that we should do it.

> *If we don't decide our goals, someone else will.*

EVERY GOOD VIKING NEEDS A CHIEF

No man is so foolish but he may sometimes give another good counsel, and no man so wise that he may not easily err if he takes no other counsel than his own. He that is taught only by himself has a fool for a master.[79]

—Ben Johnson

I believe that everyone needs a leader to follow. It doesn't matter if it's in the battlefield or the boardroom. The best leaders started by being the best followers. You can bet that back in the times of the Vikings, any guy jumping off the boat and running at the enemy alone was going to be dead meat. They needed to fight as a unit. They needed someone with a better view of the battlefield to direct them where to go. Even great warriors need a sense of humility; they need to stop themselves from always following their own instincts and learn to trust the instincts of someone with a little more experience. As for me, I've always done better when I had someone more experienced pointing the way. Whenever I hear a story about someone who has become incredibly successful, I expect to learn that the person once had a great mentor guiding and encouraging him at some point along the way. Beethoven was a pupil of Joseph Haydn, another great composer. Alexander the Great studied under Aristotle, who had been a student of Plato, another famous philosopher from ancient Greece. John C. Maxwell, author of *The 21 Irrefutable Laws of Leadership*, points out that in 1998, half of the NFL coaches can be traced back to having worked under the guidance of coaches Bill Walsh or Tom Landry.[80]

Receiving mentorship is a critical key to success. When I worked at the large automotive supplier, Rick Van Vuren was one of my original mentors in the business. He was not only my boss, he was a great guy. He influenced me and taught me a lot about people and problem solving, and he may not even know it. I want to publicly acknowledge the blessing that he has been in my life. To this day, I like to stay in touch with Rick, and I'm glad to call him a friend.

I am blessed today to be mentored by Orrin Woodward, who is currently ranked by LeadershipGurus.com as one of the top leadership gurus on earth at the time of this writing. He shares the list with other incredible authors like John Maxwell, Ken Blanchard, and Stephen Covey. Even more amazing is that he is the only leadership guru who has personally coached someone to join him on the list—that person would be my great friend and business partner Chris Brady, Orrin's coauthor on the *New York Times* bestseller *Launching a Leadership Revolution*. No other leader has helped a protégé get on the list as well, so that is impressive!

One thing that I work very hard at is being, in the words of business leader Claude Hamilton, a "passionate protégé." Every thirty days, wherever Orrin is, I will physically go out of my way to meet him. If that means buying a plane ticket, brother, I am on the plane! I value Orrin's perspective. I need to clean up my thinking and sharpen my mental saw. Orrin has achieved a level of success that I want to achieve, so I need to learn to think the way he thinks in order to get the results that he gets. It amazes and saddens me to see how many people say they want success, but then are too proud to be mentored. It is tragic.

The Value of a Mentor

My chief want in life is someone who shall make me do what I can.[81]

—Ralph Waldo Emerson

A lot of kids grow up in homes without a dad, like I did. I can't describe the sadness that this brought me. Like every young boy, I needed someone to show me the ropes, encourage me, discipline me when I messed up, and someone to cheer me on when I scored a touchdown. Our dads can be our first mentors. They are farther down the road than we may be. In time, we may realize that our dad is great at some things, but probably not great at other things, and we start to look for someone who has the answers to help us become successful in life. There are some powerful reasons we should value a mentor. Let me share some of them with you now.

- **A mentor can see the road ahead of you.** If we were walking down a path and couldn't see what was around the next corner, it would be really valuable to have someone who had a bird's-eye view shouting instructions that would warn us if we were about to step off a cliff! A mentor can warn us of what is about to happen. He has faced tough obstacles, and because of his experience, he can see when we're about to hit a land mine. Why make our own mistakes when we can learn from his experience? Proverbs 9:9 (ESV) says, "Give instruction to a wise man, and he will be still wiser: teach a righteous man, and he will increase in learning." I've made some mistakes growing up that, as a dad, I want to help my kids avoid.

117

For example, as I said before, I know at some point that my kids will probably have a buddy at school offer them beer or cigarettes. Because I'm farther down the road in life than my kids, I can see what they will eventually face and prepare them to say no before the time comes.

- **A mentor's experience can save us time.** There are two great ways of getting experience: taking our own time, which is limited, or learning from someone else. I don't know what your schedule looks like, but when I was struggling in my real estate business, I didn't have time to mess around and figure things out on my own. If Orrin had taken the time to work out the bugs on our business system, I was going to take advantage of all the effort he had made in advance. His sacrifice in going through the trial-and-error period allowed me to run even faster toward my goals. Just as Sir Isaac Newton said, "If I have seen farther than others, it is because I stood on the shoulders of giants."[82]

- **A mentor knows you are capable of more.** It's human nature to slack off and stop at the ninety-nine-yard line, just short of the winning touchdown. A mentor is the one who will shout, "Keep going!" He will push us even when we feel we've got nothing left to give. He'll challenge us to stretch ourselves. Sometimes we'll think he's nuts! And then, if we are smart enough to stop arguing and just follow his advice, we'll be amazed that he was right all along. Doubt is a tough thing to overcome, but a mentor doesn't carry around the same doubts we might because he has already done what we are trying to do. He knows it's possible. A great student can run on the confidence of his mentor and ignore his own doubt for the moment.

  In the inspirational movie *Facing the Giants*, one of the players believes that the team doesn't stand a chance against its next opponent. The coach realizes that this particular player, Brock, needs to increase his belief. He says, "I want you to do the Death Crawl, and I want to see your absolute best."[83]

Then the coach says, "I want you to go to the fifty-yard line with Jeremy on your back, but even if you can't, I want you to promise me that you are going to do your best." Brock agrees, but he doesn't seem too sure he can pull this off. "Your absolute best, Brock. And one more thing"—the coach pulls out a bandanna and blindfolds him—"I don't want you giving up at a certain point when you could have gone farther."[84]

Brock starts across the field, doing the Death Crawl. Now, for those of you who don't play football, the Death Crawl is crawling without your knees touching the ground, and Brock is doing it with a 140-pound player on his back. After a minute, Brock starts moaning and groaning. He starts complaining about how bad it hurts. And the coach keeps telling him to negotiate with his body, to keep pushing as hard as he can. "You promised me your best. Don't you quit now! It's all heart!" The coach keeps pushing him and encouraging him.[85]

Brock is in agony. He asks, "How much farther? Are we at the fifty-yard line yet?"[86]

And the coach brushes the question off. He keeps saying, "You're almost there, Brock. Just a little farther! Keep going! Don't quit! Keep going!"[87]

When Brock finally collapses in agony and exhaustion, the coach tells him to take off the blindfold. Brock is in the end zone. He has gone all the way across the field. The coach says, "Brock, you've just carried a 140-pound man across the field."[88]

And the other player chimes in, "Coach, I'm not 140 pounds—I'm 160 pounds."[89]

The coach knows that Brock has more in him than even Brock realizes.[90]

- **A mentor holds us accountable.** A lot of people perform better when they are being watched. Without someone to report to, we might play games with our integrity and not finish what we said we would. This is different from an

119

employee-boss relationship. My mentor is not my boss. It is a partnership. I listen to my mentor because I respect him. I respect his results, and I know that I am still dumb about some stuff. A mentor helps us keep our promises to ourselves. For example, if we are trying to lose weight, we might make excuses today for not getting on the treadmill. A great mentor won't accept the excuses we might give ourselves; he will remind us that we promised to accomplish something. He is a loud voice of conscience in the moments when we aren't strong. One of our goals through mentorship should be to hear something uncomfortable every time we sit down with our mentor.

> *One of our goals through mentorship should be to hear something uncomfortable every time we sit down with our mentor.*

- **A mentor sees who we could become.** We tend to notice all our flaws and weaknesses, but a mentor reminds us of what we are good at. He doesn't ignore the weaknesses; in fact, a great mentor will help us get better in the areas in which we are weak. But he will also help us if we have a bad habit of beating up on ourselves and seeing only the bad. A mentor will shine light on our gifts and our talents. We can sometimes be our own worst enemy and talk so badly to ourselves that we are defeated even before we step onto the playing field. A mentor serves as a great cheerleader during game time, helping us see that we are stronger than our negative self-talk. He believes in us when we may not believe in ourselves.

If you have the blessing of having a mentor, you want to pursue him. If Orrin says, "I can meet with you at nine o'clock on Friday night," I'm going to shift my schedule around so I'm available on Friday. Orrin's schedule supersedes mine because I'm the protégé, and he's the mentor. He doesn't need my advice; I need his. And when he says, "Be here at nine p.m.," brother, I'm parked outside at eight forty-five, doing some quick reading or replying to e-mails. I'm going to walk through that front door right at nine o'clock. I'm not going to ring his bell any earlier than that because he might be with Laurie and the kids, or reading a book, or mentoring someone else. I want to always show respect for his time. I want to get another session! It's up to me to ask Orrin, "When can we get together again?" Remember, I'm chasing Orrin to gain his wisdom, so I can get his results.

It is one thing to get some time with your mentor; it's another thing entirely to grow from it. A simple question you should ask yourself about your relationship with your mentor is: "What two or three things have I worked on since our last session?" Now, here are a couple of tougher questions for your mentor that only a true leader will ask: "Am I really listening to you? Am I truly letting you mentor me?" Make sure, by the way, that you are sitting down when you hear the answer. These might seem like tough questions, but if you really seek out an answer, it will help you.

If you are blessed to have access to a mentor, my advice is to chase him down and do whatever you can to earn time with that person. If he encourages you to read a book, buy it and read it. If he encourages you to attend a seminar that will help you learn to improve your life, I recommend you follow that advice. A simple rule in life is to find someone who has done what you want to do and follow in that person's footsteps. If you do that, you are sure to achieve your goals.

CONCLUSION

As I said earlier, being a Viking is a double-edged sword. There are some great qualities and some not-so-great qualities. Conquering new lands wasn't nearly as impressive when I had to step on other people to do it. Learning how to soften my heart toward people and show them grace literally changed my life. I know that although I have improved, I still have a lot of work to do on myself. It's great to have a little victory now and then, but the reward isn't as sweet if we've pushed aside the people we love and care about along the way. We should remind ourselves to soften our hearts toward others and be stern with ourselves, so that when we decide to sail for new lands, our friends and family will desire to join us for the journey rather than only going along because they are bound in shackles.

KEY POINTS

1. Being a Viking is a double-edged sword. I got a lot done, but I was tough on people. To truly have success in life, we must learn to show grace to others and follow the law ourselves.

2. The Vikings yearned for freedom. Those who had wealth had freedom. The same is true today.

3. The Vikings were courageous explorers. They were willing to lose sight of the shore in order to discover new lands and achieve their goals.

4. The Vikings connected communities by building bridges. Building a bridge is one of the most amazing ways of saying, "I value you, and I value our connection."

5. I would wound people with my words. My goal in using sarcasm was to tear people down so they knew I was better than they were. My bosses joked that the best way to find me was to follow the trail of bodies. That was not a compliment.

6. In order to change, we need a mentor to point out our blind spots. We can't see where we need to change.

7. Vikings have a lot of great qualities. They take action, focus on their goals, and won't let fear stand in their way.

8. We all need a mentor. A mentor can see the road ahead, save

us time, hold us accountable, and will push us to achieve our full potential. Our goal should be to hear something uncomfortable every time we sit down with our mentor.

LIVE ON RESULTS FOOD

It is no use saying, "We are doing our best." You have got to succeed in doing what is necessary.[91]

—Winston Churchill

I f hard work were all that was required to be a success, every blue-collar laborer (just as I was when I began my career) would be making a million dollars a year. Effort plays a big part in being successful, make no mistake about that. You're not going to slip out of the factory ten minutes before the whistle blows and expect to have management begging you to take a promotion. But the fact is that there are a bunch of very wealthy people who work the same amount as the minimum-wage gang, and no harder, yet they get a million times more reward for the same number of hours invested. What's up with that?

At the heart of winning comes a hunger to succeed. Something inside us craves a big victory. There has to be a gnawing, aching feeling in your gut that things must be made right in order for you to feel content, so that you'll get out there and do what it takes. This is a pretty noble feeling and I applaud people with the guts to try. But trying is not enough.

I once heard about a motivational speaker who invited an audience member up onto the stage to help him demonstrate a point. On the stage was a fold-up chair. The motivational speaker pointed to it and asked the volunteer to *"try* to pick up the chair." The man looked puzzled at the request because it seemed like a pretty easy request! The man reached over and picked up the chair.[92]

The motivational speaker said, "No, no, no, I'd like you to *try* to pick up the chair. Don't pick it up. I want you to only *try* to pick it up."

Confused, the man picked up the chair again, and then once again. The speaker said, laughing, "No! Don't pick up the chair. Just *try* to pick up the chair. You keep doing it wrong! You keep picking it up! I want you to just *try* to pick it up!"

This went back and forth a few more times with the volunteer getting increasingly confused and frustrated. Finally, the motivational speaker said, "To quote Yoda from *The Empire Strikes Back*, 'Try not. Do, or do not. There is no try.'"[93]

Missing a goal hurts inside. If someone has a gnawing aching feeling in his gut that demands that he succeed, the pain is too great to ignore. We must feast on some sort of food to try to get rid of that pain. But the type of food that satisfies us is a big key to what happens next. You see, if we just simply "try hard" to reach our goal, if we feel okay about running around, only being busy, then we are attempting to satisfy ourselves with what I call *activity food*.

A winner eventually loses his appetite for mere *activity food*. There comes a point when people who become successful find that *activity food* starts to taste pretty bland; it lacks any nutritional value in the diet of achievement. We have to reach a point where we get sick and tired of simply working hard and getting nothing to show for our effort. We are on the path to success when we are no longer satisfied with *activity food* but instead crave *results food*.

> *There comes a point when people who become successful find that activity food starts to taste pretty bland; it lacks any nutritional value in the diet of achievement.*

Robert Fritz said, "All too often, people fail to focus their choices upon results, and therefore their choices are ineffective. If you limit your choices only to what seems possible or reasonable, you disconnect yourself from what you truly want, and all that is left is compromise."[94]

These are great words of wisdom. We have to decide to be satisfied not with just effort, but with results.

> *We have to decide to be satisfied not with just effort, but with results.*

DON'T JUST BE BUSY, BE PRODUCTIVE

No steam or gas ever drives anything until it is confined. No Niagara is ever turned into light and power until it is tunneled. No life ever grows until it is focused, dedicated, disciplined.[95]
—Harry Emerson Fosdick

Orrin Woodward says, "You can't steer a parked car." What that means is that he can't coach someone who isn't at least in motion. When we are being mentored (and I hope you are), our mentor can't fix things that aren't happening. Our activity is like clay waiting to be molded into art – no clay, no art.

> *Our activity is like clay waiting to be molded into art – no clay, no art.*

Without appearing to contradict myself, let me just say that you can't be productive without *first* being busy. Get busy! Get into action! Don't sit around trying to figure out the exact perfect way to do things, and don't paralyze yourself by worrying that the activity in front of you isn't the most important task on your to-do list. Hey, if it turns out you ended up doing the second or third most important thing, at least you're getting somewhere! I am much better off racing around like a chicken with my head cut off than sitting at home doing nothing.

A mentor can help you figure out your top priorities. However, you may not have a mentor, or if you do, he probably isn't sitting on

the couch beside you each night telling you what to do next. (In fact,
any good mentor probably wouldn't
be caught dead sitting on the couch!)

> *The first step to doing the* right *thing is doing some*thing.

In those times when it's up to you to
coach yourself, you've got to resolve
that the first step to doing the *right*
thing is doing *some*thing. Once you're
in motion, you can be steered by a mentor.

Keep Pressure on Yourself

When we long for life without difficulties, remind us that oaks grow strong in contrary winds and diamonds are made under pressure.[96]

—Peter Marshall

Most people want to avoid pressure. They want life to go
easy on them. They want to relax and go fishing. I can't
blame them for that! I love fishing; it's probably my favorite pastime. However, there is a huge difference in going fishing
their way and going fishing *my* way.

"Pay now; play later" is great advice to create a wonderful life for
yourself. When I was racing to build my leadership business while
juggling a crumbling rental property "empire," I didn't do a lot of
fishing. In fact, I didn't do any. I did a lot of working and praying, and
I put the fishing on hold until I got my financial house in order. But
when you work hard *now*, you get to go fishing in style *later*.

A while back, I was driving near my home in Florida, and I saw a
beautiful new '38 Donzi fishing boat. At the time, it wasn't appropriate
for me to get it, but the boat really made an impression on me. Fast-
forward two years, and I felt it was time to put some pressure on
myself to move my business forward. In October of that year, I called
my assistant Dave and said, "I want you to sell my current fishing

boat immediately. Get rid of it. Please, get it off my land today. I don't want to see it again." I took a photo of the empty boat lift and kept the photo as the wallpaper on my phone.

Why would I do this? Most people would think I'm nuts. They'd ask, "Why torture yourself like that?" I'm strange that way, I guess. I just know my personality, and I know what buttons I need to push to get myself moving. And, brother, losing my boat was lighting a fire under me to get busy! Every time I looked at my phone, it would bug me that I hadn't hit my goal yet. All my fishing buddies were telling me how good the sharks were biting, and that was like pouring salt in my wounds. I wanted to go shark fishing so badly I could taste it!

Well, it must have been providential, because not one month later, I was driving by the same boat dealer I had passed before, and I noticed the *same* Donzi fishing boat! It looked as though it had never been touched. I felt that this boat was meant for me. I gotta tell you, I was really fired up!

After getting some advice from my mentor, I decided to put a deposit down on the boat in January of that year to secure it. I set a specific goal to hit in order to earn the new boat. It wasn't about the money—it was about finding the driver, the motivator, that would push me to do the work I needed to do. I bought the boat, but I wouldn't let myself take the boat off the lot until I hit my goal.

My friends would come by the house and say, "Hey, let's go on your new boat!"

And I would reply, "Sure, we can do that. It's sitting down at the boat dealer right now!" I actually took people down to the dealership to set foot on the boat that I owned but wouldn't use. (I need to ask the owner of the dealership if he thinks I'm crazy!)

Now, the average person would say, "To heck with it! I'm not waiting any longer; I'm going to go ahead and pick up my boat." Well, maybe that's okay for someone else, but that's just not the way I am. I like to put pressure on myself in order to perform. I'll do these weird things to torture myself in order to push myself to perform and accomplish the bigger goals.

The funny thing is, during this whole time, two other guys had tried to buy the boat, but they couldn't get financing. I don't know what their stories were, but I believe there are principles in life that will bless you in return if you honor them. I've tried to live a life of sacrificing today so I can live tomorrow, rather than borrowing today and sacrificing my tomorrow. And I'm happy to say that in April of that year, I hit my goal and picked up the boat!

It might sound like I'm contradicting myself here, but I have never really been motivated by material things. What they do provide is a *picture* of the victory, at least in my twisted mind. My wife and four children were totally on board and involved in hitting the goal. It felt great taking my boat out that first day, going sixty-five miles per hour and jumping waves and stopping to eat at one of our favorite restaurants on the famous Captiva Island. Later that day, we were off for some swimming and playing on a private beach.

I can't describe how great it felt to have earned the boat by hitting my goal, rather than just buying it on a whim (which I could have easily done). It really makes the reward so much sweeter. When you do things like this and keep pressure on yourself, you not only get a fun toy, but you combine the enjoyment of the prize with feelings of satisfaction and accomplishment. You have met your goal and maintained your principles. Is it worth paying the price for success? Yeah, it's worth it!

John W. Foster said, "One of the strongest characteristics of genius is the power of lighting its own fire."[97] You have to know how to push your own buttons. You need to have the maturity to be tough on yourself today in order to get what you really want tomorrow.

> *You need to have the maturity to be tough on yourself today in order to get what you really want tomorrow.*

Avoid Lower-Importance Tasks

Every road warrior is at a different level of performance and results. We each have a comfort zone in which we like to operate. If we stretch ourselves to lift our performance above what is currently comfortable, we can feel the pressure. But the opposite is true as well: If our performance slips below our comfort zone, we feel lousy about ourselves.

Every ninety days, my business community holds a leadership convention, and most people leave the event feeling pretty fired up. But if you don't have action steps lined up coming out of an event like that, you can slip into some negative feelings about yourself. It can be a little depressing sitting around when what we really want to do is change our lives, so sometimes we might "kill time" by just filing papers, organizing our desks, or counting paper clips.

If that's where you are, then I'm glad you're at least in motion. But the big boys aren't just running around — they are making things happen. They are leading the charge.

Sometimes some of the newer guys on my business team will report that they met with another associate in order to "pump him up" or "build the relationship." Hey, that's great, but what I'm really looking for is whether you moved the ball forward. You can meet with people a hundred times to pump them up, but the rubber meets the road when you are doing the high-importance tasks.

Never Lower the Bar on Yourself

Walking your talk is a great way to motivate yourself. No one likes to live a lie. Be honest with yourself, and you will find the motivation to do what you advise others to do.[98]

—Vince Poscente

In my business, we like to celebrate success by recognizing people who have done the work and gotten the results. We believe in an honor system and leave it up to people to tell the truth about the work they have done. Sadly, sometimes, as in any industry, people fudge the numbers and claim to have done more than they have. When they do this, they are only hurting themselves and the people around them.

Trying to live on *results food* when we are faking our results is like living on empty calories and wondering why we're still hungry! For example, if I'm trying to lose weight and faking my number of minutes on the treadmill, who am I kidding? What's the point of saying to myself, "Yeah, I did twenty minutes on the bike today," when I know I slacked off and only sat on the bike not pedaling very hard at all? What's the point of faking myself out? Every time I look in the mirror, I get an instant report card on my integrity on the bike. The truth is, you can't explain away bad results.

The famous boxer Joe Frazier says, "If you cheated on [your roadwork] in the dark of the morning, well, you're going to get found out now, under the bright lights."[99] That means that eventually, no matter what we tell other people, our real activity will be on display for the whole world to see. We can't claim to be reading people-skills books year after year and yet still continually offend people! We can't claim to listen to four to five motivational CDs each day and yet still have a miserable attitude. We can't violate biblical principles and not expect the world to find out. Honesty in our small daily actions always gets rewarded in the long run. Conversely, dishonesty in the small things will also show up in the long run.

> *Trying to live on results food when we are faking our results is like living on empty calories and wondering why we're still hungry!*

Brian Davis is a professional golfer who really understands this principle. Last year, he was playing on the PGA tour, and he was very close to winning the $1 million in prize money. But something happened that day that will stand as one of those great moments in sports that you want to teach your kids. The game had gone into sudden death, and Davis was hitting onto the green.[100]

As he executed his shot, he felt his seven iron brush against something in his backswing. He realized that he had hit a small reed. The rule in golf says that you are prohibited from "moving a loose impediment." If anyone had noticed, he would have been penalized a shot and automatically placed in second place, which meant he would lose $400,000 in prize money. Most golfers would say, "Whew! No one else noticed! I can still keep playing for the $1 million."[101]

You know what Davis did? He called himself out. He shouted for the tournament director to come over and pointed out what he had done. The tournament director was stunned at Davis's integrity, but immediately declared the match over and Davis the second-place winner.[102]

The rest of the day, Davis's phone wouldn't stop ringing. People all over the world, including golf celebrities who were his heroes, were congratulating him on the real victory—that of being honest. Who would have thought that it would make headlines for someone to have integrity and hold himself to a higher standard?[103]

I understand why Davis was motivated to do what he did. You see, at the end of the day, he would have to answer to his Father, and then he would have to answer to his son. Brian Davis wasn't just playing a game of golf that day—he was setting an example for his little boy on how to live a moral life. I aspire to be such a dad to my own kids. We should all try to hold ourselves to this kind of standard.[104]

How would you react in that circumstance? Most of us have never been put in such a position with so much on the line. I'm sure if we were asked, we would answer, "Oh, absolutely, I would do the right thing!" But so often, I see people on my business team lower the bar on themselves. I see people claim to have hit a goal, and they say to themselves, "Well, I was pretty close." And then they stand up to be recognized onstage at a leadership conference.

We should refuse to lower the bar on ourselves. I have to be tough on myself and say, "I missed that goal. I got 99 percent of the results, but not 100 percent. Next month, I'll try again. But this month, I'm calling the referee over and calling myself out. I'm telling him I missed the shot." Talent can help you reach the top, but it requires character to keep you at the top. Don't play games with integrity.

I know I am more proud of people when they admit they missed a goal—a million times more proud! And I know I really want to associate only with men who hold themselves to the same standard.

I hope you do as well.

GOING FROM PROBLEM IDENTIFIED TO PROBLEM SOLVED

Having the world's best idea will do you no good unless you act on it. People who want milk shouldn't sit on a stool in the middle of a field in hopes that a cow will back up to them.[105]
—Curtis Grant

If we ever feel that we are not making progress in business, in our jobs, or in life, it could be because we are staring a problem square in the face and doing our darndest to ignore what is staring back at us. For example, some of my friends would take me out for late dinners and gently suggest that I read the book *How to Win Friends and Influence People*. My usual response at the time was to snort and tell them the problem wasn't the rough edges in my personality but, rather, all the stupid people I kept running into! I can only shake my head now at how much I still had to learn back then – and still do!

When it comes to learning and growing, a lot of us are just entertaining ourselves with *listening* to great ideas, rather than doing the hard work of *implementing* those ideas. When we get exposed to nuggets of wisdom, we might benefit from asking ourselves some of the following questions:

- "What have I learned from this book or CD, and how can I apply this nugget of wisdom to my business or my life right now?"
- "What do I need to change about myself and my business to hit my goal?"
- To audit and improve on people skills, when walking away

from a person, one should make the effort to ask himself, "What makes me think that person likes me?"

- After delivering a business presentation, one should ask himself, "What could I have improved about my presentation tonight?"

I'm not always the sharpest knife in the drawer, but when I finally lock on to a principle, I work hard at implementing it – immediately. I feel sometimes that I have been so far behind people in terms of personal growth that my only survival technique is to grab every nugget of truth, every great idea, and put them into action.

Some people might read a life-coaching book and say, "Wow, that was a great book!" But perhaps they miss following any of the suggestions the book makes. I've come to realize that I still have so much growing and learning to do that I can't afford to miss a single lesson.

Because of this, I try really hard to follow the directions of my mentor. If you are also fortunate to have someone who takes an interest in you and your success, I would encourage you to honor that person's investment in you by passionately acting on his advice! I want the results of my mentor, and he sincerely wants me to win. So whatever my mentor suggests I do, I'm not going to waste time arguing—I'm going to do it! If my mentor said, "Tim, here's a brick wall; I need you to get to the other side," I would set about to do what he asked. I would probably take a moment and first look around to see if there was a door to use. But if there was no door or a way over, around, or under, I would put my head down and just smash a hole through the wall (not because I'm crazy, but because I trust)!

Now, maybe some other guys would stand around analyzing this problem all day long—guys who have more college degrees and a higher IQ than I do, perhaps. Maybe they would get out their tape measures and calculators and figure out how to design some sort of catapult that would launch them over the wall, or make some sort of hot air balloon to float over the wall, or build a jet pack like MacGyver to blast off and jump over the wall.

I guess I'm just too dumb to sit and analyze things to death. I'll just smash a hole in the wall with my head, look over my shoulder, and give a big smile and wave to the guys still figuring out how to do things exactly right.

Maybe I'm brash or impulsive, and that has gotten me into some hot water over the years. But taking action can produce some okay results in life. While the thinkers are thinking, the doers are getting things done!

You Have to Face Reality

One way you can spot a moving-on leader is by how well he can call himself out on his own "stuff," as well as by how open he is to other people calling him out on things. Ram Charan, author of *Execution: The Discipline of Getting Things Done*, wrote, "Realism is the heart of execution, but many organizations are full of people who are trying to avoid or shade reality. Why? It makes life uncomfortable."[106] Guess what? Life is way more uncomfortable in fantasyland!

If you want to move on in business or in life, you're going to play in the sandbox called "being uncomfortable." You've got to call a spade a spade. For example, if all the people I meet are jerks to me, and yet they get along just fine with the neighbor on the other side of the fence, chances are, they aren't the problem; *I* am!

Orrin Woodward tells the story of mentoring a group of business leaders who were struggling to move on in their businesses. Their common complaint was that a business leader they had been working with wasn't a good-enough leader and had been holding them back from achieving all that God had meant them to achieve – or so they said.

Orrin thought about this and said, "You know, the strange thing here is that I had the same business leader [at that time], and it didn't seem to slow me down. So if that variable was the same between both of us, that would mean that the business leader you are complaining about couldn't have been the problem. So your lack of success must be due to another variable. There are only two people in the equation: the business leader we are discussing and *you*. If the business leader isn't the real problem, the only other variable in the equation is . . . "

Orrin let them figure out the rest. I'm not sure those guys were too happy to have that truth grenade tossed in their direction that day! But it was necessary.

Over the years, I've had my share of moments where I figured things out the hard way. So let me share a couple of those moments with you. As you read these examples, please understand that the point I'm trying to make is that when you do finally have the little bulb go off over your head, you should take action immediately to change what you need to change. As Orrin Woodward is fond of saying, "The world is full of great ideas; what the world lacks is implementers of great ideas!" Become excellent at implementing ideas that bless your life and the lives of those around you.

From *My* Business to *Our* Business

One of the early mistakes I made in building my leadership business was that I felt very strongly that Amy's role (at least at the start) was to be at home watching the kids and that my role was to be out doing business presentations and hitting my sales goals. That might sound great on paper, but from Amy's perspective, it was getting to be a little too much to handle! Amy had three little kids under the age of six to manage, and let me tell you, it was a problem. Amy was caring for a colicky baby and had no adult conversation to look forward to. She was at her wit's end, and I was totally oblivious to it.

Poor Amy reached out to our friend and mentor Laurie Woodward, Orrin's wife, for some help in getting through to me. I was so dense I couldn't see what was going on; I was in the fight for financial survival so much that I had blinders on. I just assumed Amy would be fine with my schedule since I was doing all this hard work to benefit our family.

Laurie suggested to Amy that all four of us get together and discuss the matter. I credit Laurie for being such a great mentor to Amy and for the fact that she didn't try to solve our marital problems behind my back; instead, she included me in the discussion. I've really learned from that lesson because, even today, sometimes someone will say to me, "Tim, I want to talk with you about the problems I'm having with my wife." And I always want to make sure to involve the guy's wife in the discussion because I know she needs to be part of the solution.

Amy and I headed over to Orrin and Laurie's and sat down to chat for a bit. After Orrin got a feel for what was going on, he said, "Okay, Timbo! How about you and I go grab some Chinese food?"

We headed out, and Orrin started asking me some questions; he was trying to help me think through the situation. He asked, "So what's going on, Tim?"

I shared my point of view. In my usual bullheaded nature, I explained that I knew exactly what I was doing and that I had my role and Amy's role very clearly figured out. I did the work, and Amy raised the kids (alone). I was out building the business as fast as I could, and I really thought Amy was better off managing the home. I really couldn't see why she was having such a hard time.

He gently asked, "Tim, where did you come up with the idea to leave Amy at home all week with the kids?"

I shrugged and, not realizing how foolish I would sound later, I said, "Well, I thought it up myself!"

Orrin said, "Oh." And then he paused to let me think about what I had just said.

After a moment, I realized what he was getting at; when he saw that I got it, we both laughed, and he slapped me on the knee.

Orrin's point was that I was taking my own advice, rather than seeking advice from someone who had more experience in the same situation with four kids! Orrin had been down that road already, but I was really struggling; therefore, it would make sense that I could learn from him if I would just listen.

When he suggested that I make a change, I went home and made the change. I talked to Amy, and together we came up with the plan to hire babysitters. Now, here is the big point of this whole story: When a mentor offers advice, we should act on it right away – not a month from now, *right* now. We can judge how good we are as students by how fast we implement our mentor's advice. I feel we should always, always want to be great students.

By the way, I'm not talking about following someone blindly around as if he were a seeing-eye dog. I have a great amount of respect for my mentor, and I trust his insight. The issues I personally work on are not

> *We can judge how good we are as students by how fast we implement our mentor's advice.*

the point; but the "spirit of the law," if you can appreciate this, is that I am always working hard on trying to improve, and I think we can all improve in some way in that regard.

If You're Happy, Remember to Inform Your Face

In my early years of learning to build a people business (and even still today), it helped me to remember that people prefer to work with people they know, like, and trust. And a great way to open the door to all three of those things quite quickly is to simply smile.

One of the beauties of life is that a smile is a universally understood gesture. It was amazing to me that some of the most beautiful smiles I've ever seen came from the people in Haiti, where I traveled this last year on a mission trip. The people there, who seemingly had so little to smile about by American standards, had the brightest smiles. It doesn't matter if you are in Haiti or Hawaii or Houston—everywhere you go, every culture recognizes what a smile is and values it. Smiling tells people that we like them, that we are friendly and approachable, and that we are not a threat; in business, it tells people that we deserve to win the sale.

So, what did Tim "the Viking" do? In a nutshell, I didn't smile. Smiling might have caused my face to crack. Clearly, if I had ever risked smiling, that would have been the end of me.

It's not that I didn't know that smiling was probably a good idea; it's that I was really under so much stress that I couldn't bear to pretend I was happy. I felt like my heart was being crushed from the stress. We were three months behind on our mortgage, in danger of losing houses every day from my real estate business, and Amy was getting denied at the grocery store checkout because of insufficient funds. It felt like I was waging war. I was trying so hard to hold everything together that the cracks in my personality were glaring. I just didn't feel like I had a lot to smile about.

Both Orrin Woodward and Chris Brady, on separate occasions, had taken me aside and told me, "Tim, you've got to be more inviting to people. If you are happy, please notify your face!" Orrin recommended that I read another great book *How to Have Confidence and Power in Dealing with People*. This book taught me the three As: accept, approve, and appreciate. And, along with Dale Carnegie's great book *How to Win Friends and Influence People*,[107] this book taught me to remember to smile.[108]

Orrin didn't give up on me. He has this incredible ability to see the good inside people, to see the leader waiting to emerge—even when guys like me sometimes struggle to see what he's talking about. Orrin said, "Tim, you're so results focused. Always remember: The real result in almost any business is building relationships. Don't count how many people choose to sign the dotted line. Measure how many people would go into battle with you."

I realized he was right. Orrin suggested that I be more inviting at meetings: Greet new people as they walk in, welcome them, and make them feel comfortable. He also suggested that I start playing around and having more fun with my team – while smiling! After all, our business team has three rules:

1. Have fun.
2. Make money.
3. Make a difference.

I want to encourage you to act quickly on your mentor's advice. Not only is it a sign of respect to him, showing you recognize the truth in his counsel, but it also shows you appreciate his taking the time to help you. Decide to be the very best person you know at going from problem identified to problem solved!

Execute That Frog!

It is amazing how few oil people really understand that you only find oil if you drill wells. You may think you're finding it when you're drawing maps and studying logs, but you have to drill.[109]

—John Masters

Ralph Waldo Emerson said, "Good thoughts are no better than good deeds, unless they be executed."[110] When I say, "Execute that frog" (with apologies to Brian Tracy and his book *Eat That Frog!*), I mean we should attack our goals and get things done. I can stare out the window all day long, imagining how great life is going to be once I finally get moving, but eventually, I need to put some daylight between the seat and my rear end. After you've taken care of the "Ready" and "Aim" parts of your plan, there comes a point where you simply have to get busy and pull the trigger. Here are three critical steps to consider when moving ahead to accomplish your goals.

First, Get Busy on Your Top Goals

Action expresses priorities.[111]

—Charles A. Garfield

A properly defined goal explains, "From what to what and by when?" Once you have defined your goals, you must determine which ones are your top priorities. In his book

Good to Great, author Jim Collins uses another term; he asks, "What are your BHAGs, or Big Hairy Audacious Goals?"[112] Whatever you call these big goals, you'd better have them!

The authors of the book *Influencer* cite one company that is brilliant at focusing on its BHAG: Southwest Airlines. Its focus is "to be *the* low-cost airline." Whenever a proposal comes up to make a change, Southwest's leaders just ask, "Does this help us keep our position as the low-cost airline?" If someone suggests, "Hey, let's add some gourmet food to the menu," then they will shoot down the suggestion. Although it might be a wonderful idea, it won't help them with their BHAG of being *the* low-cost airline.[113]

One of the most important things about having main goals is realizing you can't have fifty-seven different goals. If everything is a priority, then nothing is a priority! It's like using a highlighter while you read to remember your favorite parts

> *If everything is a priority, then nothing is a priority!*

of the book. If you highlight everything, then really, you're just saying that everything is the best part of the book!

We have to pick just a couple of key things that we are going to focus on. Author Brian Tracy suggests taking thirty seconds and asking yourself what your top three goals are. If you have only thirty seconds, you can't write down one hundred goals — only the top three. Doing this little exercise forces you to pick what you care about the most.[114]

Maybe you have a business goal of selling one hundred homes this year in your real estate company. Maybe you have a goal of getting back to a thirty-four-inch waist. Maybe you have decided you're going to write a book. Maybe you have a goal to read a book! (Well, I guess you are already doing that!) These are all great goals. Just remember that every goal you take on is now competing for your time, your physical energy, your money, and your mental energy.

If we spread ourselves too thin with too many goals, we end up giving a half-hearted effort on twelve different tasks, and we don't finish anything. You have to get some practice in saying *no* to good goals so that you can only say *yes* to the best goals, as we've discussed before.

One guy who was great at saying no to good ideas was the late Steve Jobs, founder and president of Apple Inc. You might think, "Tim, I thought this guy was really passionate about creating the most amazing and innovative gadgets—doesn't that mean he says yes to a lot of goals?" That would seem logical, except it's the exact opposite.

Steve Jobs was notorious at Apple Inc. for turning down good ideas. People constantly approached him with suggestions on how to improve this widget over here and how to streamline this concept over there. Steve Jobs would thank them and then blow the idea away. He'd say no to a thousand good ideas so that he could say yes to one *amazing* idea.[115]

In fact, in 1998, Apple had 350 products. Jobs famously came back to the sinking company and cut the product line down to ten items. He wanted ten world-class, game-changing products, and having 350 mediocre ideas was standing in the way. You and I can learn from that example. We have to be just as ruthless on ourselves when whittling down our list of top priorities. Hack through them with a machete and clear out the thick weeds. Get your priority list down to two or three key things and focus all your efforts on those.[116]

Second, Focus on Vital Behaviors

If you continually ask yourself, "What's important now?," you won't waste time on the trivial.[117]

—Lou Holtz

Most people track their progress by looking in the rear-view mirror! What do I mean by that? They look at what has been accomplished in the past, either good or bad. The problem is, if you want to live in the future, you need to focus on the future. I don't ever want to be a *has-been*; I want to be a *gonna-be*.

143

Let's say, for example, your job is in sales and you want to make $5,000 in commissions one week. Perhaps that equals ten sales at $500 of profit for you. The vital behavior to watch may be the number of sales presentations you give. You decide that's the key factor that you can control to drive you toward your goal.

Now, you might get even more specific and ask, "What's the vital behavior that controls the number of sales presentations I make?" Suppose you decide you need to make at least four presentations a week. The vital behavior that controls the number of presentations you book would be how many prospects you call to schedule appointments. If you are calling a couple of people and getting voice mails, you need to focus on the vital behavior: Increase your number of phone calls. That increases the number of people you reach and the number of appointments you successfully schedule, which increases the number of presentations you deliver, and the amount of money you will earn will skyrocket.

It seems like pretty simple stuff, but I am amazed at how many people don't do simple planning. Most people spend more time planning their wedding than they spend planning their marriage, and they spend more time planning Christmas parties and shopping for toys than they spend understanding the real meaning of Christmas (and I don't mean Santa Claus). Don't look at an empty calendar just wishing for sales appointments — take action on the vital behaviors!

Third, Create a Culture of Positive Peer Pressure

Don't make friends who are comfortable to be with. Make friends who will force you to lever yourself up.[118]

—Thomas J. Watson

One of the greatest success stories in American business is Walmart. Sam Walton was an absolute visionary, and he wasn't an ivory-tower leader: He got his hands dirty by visiting as many stores as he could. Every Saturday morning, he would meet with the managers to review their scoreboards. Although he didn't use that term, he would spend all night looking at the numbers, getting ready for that meeting, so he knew firsthand how each store was performing.[119]

I can't imagine how it would feel if I was one of those managers sitting in that meeting with an underperforming store! I imagine I'd be squirming in my seat, waiting for Sam to say, "Hey, Tim, how's that store going?" I'd know he could see all the numbers and that he probably spent all night looking at every part of my business on paper. It would not be a fun moment because I'd be sitting in front of all my peers, and I'd have to explain why I hadn't come through. I know multimillionaires who have been wealthy for years and still operate the same way.

Peer pressure is a powerful motivator! We tend to care what our peers think. If we hang around high-performing people, we get uncomfortable if we're not running fast enough to keep up with the pack. I know if I faced such public accountability that I would run as hard as I could to make sure that I had some great results to talk about when my turn came to share.

Tony Robbins, a famous motivational speaker and author, was invited to speak before a group of marines. After the presentation, the general was driving Tony back to the airport, and Tony remarked on what a wonderful group of soldiers he commanded.[120]

"But, Tony," the general sighed, "it saddens me that these guys are in such amazing shape, probably the best shape they've been in their whole lives! They have more mental toughness, more stamina and confidence than they've probably ever had, and what I see over and over is that when these guys go home and get away from this group of men, they will slack off. They will slip back into their bad habits, lose a lot of what they've gained, and gain a lot of weight. I just don't understand why this happens!"[121]

Tony Robbins thought about it for

> *We rise to the level of expectations of our peer group.*
> *– Tony Robbins*

a moment and answered, "We rise to the level of expectations of our peer group."[122]

That is a profound statement. If we are hanging around high-performing people, we rise to their expectations. If not, then the opposite happens. So what does a high-performing team expect from one another? They expect the best. When we are left to our own devices, we are weak and might give in to our own excuses.

Track-and-field Olympian Jesse Owens said:

> There is something that can happen to every athlete, every human being—it's the instinct to slack off, to give in to the pain, to give less than your best . . . the instinct to hope to win through luck or your opponent's not doing their best, instead of going to the limit and past your limit, where victory is always to be found. Defeating those negative instincts that are out to defeat us is the difference between winning and losing, and we face that battle every day of our lives.[123]

For me, I know it helps to be held accountable by my mentor and my peers. It keeps me going when I'm tired or feeling beat up and discouraged. Just knowing that the guys I respect are watching me keeps me pushing myself a little longer and a little harder. But more importantly, I'm accountable to Tim Marks and to my Creator. I am often puzzled when the people I mentor say things like, "I just need you to hold me accountable." While it is good to have an accountability partner, it has to begin with the man in the mirror.

So my challenge to you is this: Identify what your main goals are. Figure out what vital behaviors you need to focus on to accomplish them. Then create a culture of positive peer pressure to generate top performance. Following these steps is a great road map to success in business and in life.

GETTING IT DONE

You can't aim a duck to death.[124]

—Gael Boardman

While I was talking with some business partners in Toronto, Canada, I heard about the slogan on the side of a police car: "Deeds speak." Indeed. Your actions create your reality. I can't be a jerk to my wife and expect any-

> *Deeds speak.*
> *— York Region Police Slogan*

thing other than the cold shoulder in return. I might say the words "*I love you*" all day long, but it won't matter much if I have been cruel. There really isn't a magic formula to success in business or in life. You simply need to define what you want, learn what you need to learn, and do what you need to do.

I've seen people change the process of "dream, struggle, victory" to "scheme, grumble, misery." Scheming means that we try to manipulate the situation and the details. We avoid our responsibilities and hope someone else handles the workload for us. When we know we aren't doing what we should, we start to grumble and make excuses about the poor results we are achieving. But grumbling doesn't create results — it creates misery. If we use the formula of "scheme, grumble, misery," we will end up living a *settle-for life*, rather than a life of excellence.

I've heard that you can make a million excuses or a million dollars, but you can't make both. I agree with that sentiment, but I think we can improve upon it. You see, I've watched people give up on a million dollars because of one excuse, and I've watched people earn a million dollars when they only had one big reason (and many reasons they should *not* have succeeded, but chose to anyway).

Sometimes we offer excuses as to why we didn't hit a goal. In my own business, I teach leaders a very specific strategy. It's like a successful play in a football team's playbook. That strategy, or "play," is called time and time again; it works every time, and I never need to change it. But I bump into some people who don't execute that play for whatever reason. They ask me, "Tim, what's the *new* thing that we're going to do?"

I explain that as long as the play keeps working, it's what we're going to do. Some people don't like that. Sam Truslow, senior member at California design firm IDEO, said, "When people want new ideas, what they are really saying is that they can't execute."[125]

Some associates I've worked with belong to the idea-of-the-month club. They hop from one idea to the next. If they would focus on executing the plan that works, they wouldn't waste so much time on things that don't. The problem is they never settle on the single *great* idea that will propel their business forward. In his book *Outliers*, author Malcolm Gladwell says that mastery requires ten thousand hours of practice.[126] Yet you can't reach the ten thousand hours of practice required for mastery if you spend one hundred hours on one idea, then one hundred hours on the next idea, and so on. You need to settle on the one "hedgehog" principle, as Jim Collins describes in *Good to Great*, and get good at that.[127]

Marketing guru Seth Godin discusses the idea of executing your goal. He has coined the term *shipping* to describe what is happening. In his book *Linchpin*, Godin quotes Steve Jobs, then president of Apple Inc. as saying, "You gotta ship."[128] What this means is that you have to get your product or service out the door and en route to the customer. Making the product and staring at the product are great, but the key is to get it out the door. Always be willing to do whatever amount of work you are required to do to finish executing your task.

You Get What You Expect

I never expect to lose. Even when I'm the underdog, I still prepare a victory speech.[129]

—H. Jackson Brown Jr.

We don't often get what we want, or (thankfully) what we deserve, but we tend to get what we picture and expect. In sales, your closing ratio will go up when your expectations go up. Many of the business leaders I coach have all the talent and skills required in their field, but what they sometimes struggle with is seeing themselves getting the prize. You have to *believe*. When you chase a goal, you have to get your subconscious mind so fired up, so stinking excited, that you really feel as if you've already accomplished the goal, and you have to be jumping up and down because you're so excited!

Walt Disney famously visualized his Epcot Center theme park in Orlando before he passed away. Bill Gates visualized having a computer with his Microsoft software on it on every desktop. Billy Durant, founder of General Motors, visualized that the United States would one day have massive freeways that crisscrossed the nation. Stephen Spielberg visualized becoming a Hollywood director. In his new book *Resolved*, Orrin Woodward tells the story of how Peter Vidmar visualized winning the gold medal in gymnastics.[130] In each of these examples, each person got exactly what he expected.

Olympic athletes have been doing this for years. In the 1984 Olympics in Los Angeles, a sixteen-year-old gymnast named Mary Lou Retton scored a perfect ten in her routine and won the gold medal. What a lot of people don't know is that just six weeks earlier, she injured her knee and required surgery on it. She would lie in bed visualizing her routine at night. She would vividly imagine hitting the equipment, the smell of the dust, the roar of the crowd as she moved perfectly. She even imagined the sound of "The Star Spangled Banner" echoing throughout the arena. She saw herself landing perfectly and

149

scoring a ten. She imagined it over and over in her mind, and she made it come true.[131]

If you expect to win, you're going to push yourself to the last mile. You'll make one last sales call to a prospect. You'll run one more lap on the track. Simply visualizing success doesn't make it happen. As I have said already, you have to be willing to work hard. But getting a goal clear in your mind and determining to attain it is an essential ingredient in your motivation to put in the work that is necessary. If you've already decided you're going to lose, then you've lost. The biggest battle we face isn't against our competitors—it's against our own doubt.

> *The biggest battle we face isn't against our competitors - it's against our own doubt.*

Don't tell yourself about what held you back before. Don't list the reasons why you failed in the past. Don't tell yourself how much better the competition is, or how you don't have the right tools or procedures. Take all that junk and chuck it out. If you have that garbage running around in your head—and I say this with love—cast it off! Tell yourself, "I'm going to win. I already have won. I'm just waiting to claim my trophy! It's already done!" You just need to believe it will come together and see yourself claiming that gold medal, and, brother, you will! This all sounds strange to us "normal" people who have not won an Olympic gold medal, but this is what it takes.

Excuses Are Useless

Excuses are the nails used to build a house of failure.[132]
—Don Wilder and Bill Rechin

I've met far too many people who don't want to do the hard work of improving themselves. "You can't teach an old dog new tricks," they grumble loudly to whoever will listen. Making that statement is like asking the "chicken or the egg?" question. Whenever I hear someone complain that they can't change, I wonder to myself,

"Which came first—becoming an old dog, or refusing to learn new tricks?" I believe that when you're through changing, you're through. (More specifically, change is inevitable, but growth must be pursued.)

> *It doesn't matter if it's hard to change; it only matters if you should change.*

You see, it doesn't matter if it's *hard* to change; it only matters if you *should* change. Famed broadcast journalist Edward R. Murrow once said, "Difficulty is the excuse that history never accepts."[133] It didn't matter that it was hard for me to soften my rough edges; it was necessary. It didn't matter that it was hard for me to give up my alcoholism; it was necessary. It didn't matter that it was hard to be engaged as a husband and a father; it was necessary.

> *Difficulty is the excuse that history never accepts.*
> *— Edward R. Murrow*

In fact, just take the whole idea of "it's hard" and chuck it out. Whenever something is noble, righteous, honorable, morally sound, affirming, and built on biblical principles, then, as Nike says, "just do it."

The statement "it's hard" is a poor man's excuse for mediocrity because everything exceptional is hard. If it were easy, it wouldn't be the exception, it would just be the norm.

> *The statement "it's hard" is a poor man's excuse for mediocrity because everything exceptional is hard.*

Every worthwhile endeavor invites disaster along the way. Every grand idea invites ridicule. Every brave stand on an issue invites controversy. Every commitment means saying no to the good so you can say yes to the best. None of this is easy. Stop looking for easy and start going after worthwhile.

As my good friend Jim Martin says, "Excuses are like belly buttons - everyone's got one, and they don't do anything!" Excuses don't generate revenue, create solutions, or produce energy. They can't protect you later from the results of poor choices. If you choose not to put on your seat belt and then end up in a fatal accident, you can't stand at the Pearly Gates and debate the issue—you're dead! Saying "The dog ate my homework" carries the same credibility at the age of forty-five as it did at the age of five.

Here are three solid reasons why you need to cast off any excuses that are holding you back in life:

- **Excuses create a psychological barrier.** Most of the time, our biggest barrier to success isn't the world around us—it's our own limiting thinking. As soon as we tell ourselves, "I can't hit my goal because . . . ," we're already beaten. We have to learn to smash those mental barriers so they don't hold us back, and a great way to do so is to study the stories of people who have succeeded at things we once thought were impossible.

  One such example is that of Benoit Lecomte, a French-born resident of Austin, Texas, who achieved one of the greatest athletic feats of all time. It had long been thought that it was utterly impossible to swim across the Atlantic Ocean. But at the age of thirty-two, Lecomte became the first man to do it. The loss of his father to colon cancer in 1992 inspired him to attempt a barrier-shattering example of endurance the world had never before seen and which many had never imagined possible.[134]

  To raise money for research to combat colon cancer, he resolved to swim from the shores of Cape Cod to Quiberon, France. He engaged high-performance coaches to guide him through the grueling preparation for his adventure, swimming and cycling for hours every day for two years.[135]

  On July 16, 1998, he set out with only a small support team on a forty-foot sailboat just ahead of him. He braved bad weather, frigid waters, unrelenting exhaustion, an arm injury, and fear. At one point, Lecomte watched in terror as a great white shark followed him underwater, just thirty feet below his position. It was held at bay only by the protective field of electromagnetic signals that his sailboat emitted, which were designed to ward off such predators.[136]

Seventy-two days after having begun his trek, utterly spent emotionally and physically, he collapsed victorious on the beaches of France on September 28, 1998. His example shattered a mental and physical barrier that many an excuse had kept standing for centuries.[137]

- **Excuses erode your confidence the next time you need to take action.** Since the greatest antidote to fear is action, it makes sense that anything that causes inaction is going to sap your confidence. Excuses are like acid to your ambitions. It can be pretty easy to make up reasons to give in to laziness or cowardice.

If you need to stand up and give a presentation at work and you are scared of public speaking, you might try to mask your fear with what *sounds* like a pretty valid reason to take a pass. "I don't own the right graphics software to make an impressive presentation," you might tell yourself.

If a young man wants to ask a girl's father for permission to take his daughter out on a date but doesn't have a lot of self-confidence, he might make excuses for not trying. "I'll need to get the time off of work to go out, and my boss really needs my help right now."

If you feel you've put on weight but keep putting off going to the gym, you might get home and think, "The kids haven't had enough time with me this week, and little Billy needs me to help him with his math homework. "(This is fine, but not if it's used as an excuse.)

If a husband needs to admit a mistake he has made to his wife, he might tell himself, "She's been so busy lately. I'll just wait a few more weeks – no use having a courageous conversation when she's feeling run-down."

All these explanations might sound perfectly reasonable if the real reason that you weren't taking action wasn't actually something else. The more out of practice you get with taking action, the harder it becomes to dust off the cobwebs. You can't lie to yourself and still expect to win in life. Robert Brault said, "Success is a tale of obstacles overcome, and for every obstacle overcome, an excuse not used."[138]

- **Excuses teach your friends and family that they should make excuses, too.** Not only do excuses erode your dreams, they erode the dreams of those around you. Every time you give in to your weakness, you give the people around you a get-out-of-jail-free card to imitate your bad example. When you snap at your spouse and shrug it off by saying, "It's not my fault; I've had a long day," you've just told everyone that a bad attitude is a matter of circumstance, not choice. Every one of us sets an example for those around us, whether we want the responsibility or not. But especially when you are a parent, those little eyes are watching you and counting on you to point them in the right direction.

One powerful example of a family member inspiring the best in others is that of Patrick Henry Hughes. When he was born, the delivering physician immediately noticed Patrick was afflicted with a rare genetic disorder, and what would have normally been a moment of joy for his parents quickly turned into a moment every parent dreads. The doctor delivered the grim news: Patrick would be unable to have full use of his arms and legs, leaving him permanently confined to a wheelchair his entire life. But the most heartbreaking discovery was that Patrick was born without eyes. He would never have the ability to see.[139]

Patrick's father was a religious man, but in this moment, even his strong faith was tested. He struggled with the same questions many of us might ask in a similar situation: Why had God chosen to do this? What part of God's plan could this possibly be? Was this punishment, or a gift? "Why my son, Lord?" he asked. In time, the answer would inspire him.[140]

Almost by accident, Patrick's dad discovered his son had an amazing talent. One day while he was playing the piano with Patrick seated on his lap, the boy's little arms and hands reached out, found their way to the keys, and began to repeat the simple melody he had heard. By his second birthday, he could tap out a song at request. Patrick was playing blues by high school, and by the time he reached university, his musical reputation preceded him.[141]

As soon as he arrived at the University of Louisville, the band director sought him out and encouraged him to do what seemed impossible—join the marching band. Patrick laughed. "How can I be a part of the marching band when I can't even walk?" he wondered.[142]

Without hesitation, his dad had the answer. He said, "If my son Patrick is passionate about joining the marching band, then I'll do my part, too!" So Patrick's dad rearranged his work schedule to begin working the graveyard shift for UPS, keeping his afternoons free. He joined the University of Louisville marching band with Patrick. He now works from eleven o'clock at night until six in the morning, sleeps till lunchtime, and wakes up to join his son at school. Each game day, they walk onto the playing field as a united team, with Patrick manning the trumpet and his dad maneuvering the wheelchair for him. They attend every practice together, with Patrick's dad hustling to follow the formation along with the other players. Their commitment inspires each other. In a situation such as theirs, it would be easy to make excuses. Instead, they've made their circumstances a reason to excel and have inspired countless numbers of people in the process.[143]

I could probably list fifty more reasons not to make excuses, but I trust you're already sold on the point. If you truly want to achieve all your dreams and really win in the game of life, there is no place for making excuses. For every setback you have faced, someone has faced a situation ten times worse and created ten times more success. Even a casual survey of success stories would give you the mental ammunition to know that if other people have suffered greatly and overcome, you can, too. If other people have pushed themselves to become the best they can be, why can't you?

If you're going to change, you need to drop the excuses. If you want to lose weight, save your marriage, improve your career, better your financial situation, ensure your business success, or change your attitude, you have to stop selling yourself on the reasons why you can't do it. If you keep making excuses, you get to keep them. If you're going to make an excuse as to why you're not successful, make it a good one because you're going to have to live with it for the rest of your life.

> If you're going to make an excuse as to why you're not successful, make it a good one because you're going to have to live with it for the rest of your life.

The Speed of the Leader Is the Speed of the Group

Example has more followers than reason. We unconsciously imitate what pleases us and approximate to the characters we most admire.[144]

—Christian Nestell Bovee

High-performing teams tend to start with high-performing leaders. If a leader is a bump-on-a-log, leading through position or intimidation, any high-performing leaders on his team are probably looking past that manager and looking with an eye toward gaining the respect and attention of a better-qualified leader higher up the ladder.

If we are ever dissatisfied with how our team is performing—whether it is our team at work, at church, on the sports field, or even our family "team"—we should never point the finger at the other people involved. We should always have a conversation with the leader in the mirror and ask, "What more could I have done, and what more can I do now?"

Bill Hybels says:

Speed of the leader, speed of the team. If you cannot say "Follow me" to your followers—and mean it—then you've got a problem, a big one. Follow my values. Follow my integrity. Follow my work ethic, my commitment, and my communication patterns. Fight as I fight. Focus as I focus. Sacrifice as I sacrifice. Love as I love. Repent as I repent. Admit wrong as I admit wrong. Endure hardship as I endure hardship. When requisite actions back them up, these are the words that set followers' hearts soaring.[145]

> *Fight as I fight. Focus as I focus. Sacrifice as I sacrifice. Love as I love. Repent as I repent. Admit wrong as I admit wrong. Endure hardship as I endure hardship.*
> *— Bill Hybels*

Bill offers some great advice. We can't expect more from people than we are willing to do ourselves. People always learn from our example, whether it's a good one or otherwise. If we cut corners, slack off, take a sick day, skip work or cut out early, leave a trail of broken promises, talk behind people's backs, or steal glory and shift blame, then we shouldn't be surprised if the people we lead start to imitate our bad behavior! (This is especially true at home!)

However, on the flipside, we should not expect anyone to perfectly copy our great behavior. We might do things just perfectly for a few weeks in an effort to "whip" our team into shape, and then we might get upset if they don't do what we want! I learned a long time ago that the people we lead will tend to do 50 percent of what we do right, and 100 percent of what we do wrong. People don't do what *we* want— they do what *they* want. I can't tell people, "Be in the office at eight a.m.," and then roll in at nine thirty in the morning and expect them to be there, let alone get angry if they aren't! I would be an absolute hypocrite. Good leaders would never say, "Do as I say and not as I do." Rather, good leaders would say, "I'll show you how!"

Do you want your pack to start running harder? Be the lead dog, baby. Get moving! Whatever we hope our group does, we should plan on doing twice as much. If we want our business team to do fifteen business presentations a month, we should gear up to do thirty. If a man wants his kids to speak respectfully to their mom, he should treat his wife as if she is a queen. If we want our people to read a positive book each month, we should be willing to read two. If we want a fast-moving group, then we should decide to be a fast-moving leader.

Do It Now: Overcoming Procrastination

Today's greatest labor-saving device is tomorrow.[146]
—Woodrow Wilson

I love Brian Tracy's book *Eat That Frog!* I bought that book eight years ago, and like so many people, I took a few weeks getting around to reading it. The irony is that the book is about procrastination![147]

Procrastination is one of our biggest obstacles in getting things done. Results come from taking action, not from sitting around wishing that things will get better. So many of us are waiting for all the stoplights to turn green before we begin the journey toward our goals. We shouldn't use that as an excuse not to begin. Napoleon Hill, author of *Think and Grow Rich*, says, "Do not wait, the time will never be 'just right.' Start where you stand, and work with whatever tools you may have at your command, and better tools will be found as you go along."[148]

Here's the mental game that most of us play to procrastinate: We don't want to feel bad about avoiding something, especially when we believe we should do what we're thinking about. So to avoid feeling bad because we avoided taking action (there's a brain teaser for you!), we say to ourselves, "I haven't said I won't do this task. In fact, I've said I will! All I'm saying is that I'll do it tomorrow."

That's a great way to lie to ourselves and avoid reality. The reality is that deep down, we know if we play these little mental games with ourselves, we're really just saying, "I'm not going to do it."

Here's what's going on inside my head when I am procrastinating: "Whatever I am supposed to do, I feel like doing it now will be really unpleasant, and doing it later will feel a whole lot better." That's it! That's all procrastination is.

So the way around procrastination is really, really simple. In fact, it's so obvious that as soon as I say it, you'll realize you already knew this answer. However, I should warn you that while the answer is simple, it may not be at all comfortable. As an example, bench-pressing three hundred pounds is simple. You just lie on the bench, put your hands on the bar, and push up. However, while doing that might be simple, it definitely isn't easy.

Here's what you do: Make it really uncomfortable to *not* do the task and really rewarding if you *do* the task. How do you do that? You add some rewards and consequences. For example, let's say you need to clean out the garage, but you keep putting it off. Use this very simple strategy: Pick something you really enjoy and resolve that you can't have it or do it until the task is complete. Let's suppose you love going to the movies and the latest summer blockbuster opens this week. Tell yourself, "I don't get to go to the movies again until that garage is cleaned." After you miss the opening weekend, you'll start wishing you could just go to that movie, and then you'll *want* to do some spring cleaning!

Make sure that the size of the reward is appropriate for the effort involved in doing the task. Sometimes we might make the mistake of setting too *high* a reward for too *small* a task. We might say, "I get to make a large purchase like a new television or indulge in a shopping spree after I have cleaned out the garage." Those might be fine rewards, but to me, they seem a little too big for the task involved.

Here's another example: Let's say you need to make some important phone calls but you keep putting them off. If you want to go hard-core, you can say, "Okay, I have to take ice-cold showers every single morning until I finish making all of these business calls!" If you've ever been afraid of making phone calls, it's amazing how this little trick will get you running!

I have a great friend and business partner in California. He had a very specific goal he needed to hit. In order to stay focused on it, he resolved he would not have any fried food until the goal was complete. (And he loves fried food!) At the same time, his wife decided she wouldn't have any chocolate until they hit their business goal. So you appreciate how big a sacrifice this was for her; she loves chocolate. (She might even literally have dreamt about chocolate!) All of a sudden, they got very busy to hit their business goals because they wanted to have their rewards together!

Here's a great point Brian Tracy makes in *Eat That Frog!*: Rather than be addicted to chicken or movies, why don't you become addicted to the positive feeling of getting things done?

> This habit of starting and completing important tasks has an immediate and continuous payoff; you feel a surge of energy, enthusiasm, and self-esteem. This triggers the release of endorphins in your brain. This gives you a natural "high." You can actually develop a "positive addiction" to endorphins and to the feeling of enhanced clarity, confidence, and competence that they trigger.[149]

Winners get things done. Learn to get past whatever is holding you back. Learn to push your own buttons and get yourself to do what you know you should. When you learn these techniques, you'd be amazed at what you can accomplish!

Start Your "Seven-Day Sprint"

Don't be fooled by the calendar. There are only as many days in the year as you make use of. One man gets only a week's value out of a year while another man gets a full year's value out of a week. [150]

—Charles Richards

Stephen Covey wrote a powerful book called *First Things First*. In it he describes a great way to think about how to schedule your priorities. Covey suggests we try to plan our priorities around a weekly focus. [151]

Most of us can't touch on all of our priorities each day; for example, it might not be realistic to go to the gym for an hour every day. But it's probably realistic to think about going a few times over the course of the week. Another example would be night school: If you are working on your MBA, most people might be able to carve out one or two nights a week to attend night school from seven to ten p.m. But it might be unrealistic to plan on going every night.

To manage all of your priorities, think about all you can do in one week. You are going to need time to renew your spirit, to attend church and worship if you are a person of faith (which I would encourage that you become), to play with your kids, and to go on a date with your spouse. In a perfect week, I'm going to carve out time to read from good books; to listen to motivational CDs; to exercise; and, weather permitting, to go fishing. As well as all of these things, there are very specific weekly business goals that my business leaders and I focus on.

Whatever your goal may be, think about living seven days of excellence in a row. Imagine how proud you will feel when you make a personal promise and keep your integrity with that leader staring back at you in the mirror. Imagine seven days of following a diet plan perfectly and doing a set of push-ups in the morning. Perhaps it's seven days in a row of turning off the television and reading a positive book. Maybe it's studying each day for your upcoming business exam. I know I feel great when I uphold the commitments I've made

161

to myself!

In our business, we teach our leaders to do a *minimum* of four business presentations a week. Anything less, and people just don't get the results for which they are looking. To visualize a fun example of a scoreboard to track this concept, imagine the dashboard on your Bentley displaying the RPMs. If your goal is to do four to six business presentations that week, imagine keeping your RPM hovering between 4000 and 6000 RPM.

One key difference with this dashboard is that the colors are *reversed*: Any activity level *below* 4000 RPM will drift toward the redline, and any activity *above* 4000 RPM is guiding us toward the green! If we have a goal of doing four to six business presentations a week, this is a great mental image for us to keep score on whether we are doing enough business presentations that week to deserve the results we desire. This same example could be used for health. For example, just replace "business" with "fitness" and replace "presentations" with "miles run" or "minutes exercising."

Each week, we need to shake off the cobwebs, dust ourselves off from any disappointments or setbacks, rev up our engines, and sprint for seven days. Seven days to hit each of our goals in all eight key areas of our lives: faith, finance, fitness, family, fun, friendship, freedom, and following. By sprinting hard for seven days, we can have success in every area of our lives!

CONCLUSION

No one understands that you have given everything. You must give more.[152]

—Antonio Porchia

There are no awards for "close enough," except in tossing horseshoes and hand grenades. Remembering your wedding anniversary only a day late is pretty close to being correct, but you probably won't like the reaction waiting for you. Having "tried hard" to study for a medical exam won't cut it when it comes time to hand out the passing grades.

With an ocean of opportunity before us, we need to be dissatisfied with just treading water. At a certain point, we need to start paddling toward our goals and reaching them. Don't be too hard on yourself if you've been snacking on *activity food* for a while. If your self-esteem has taken a beating because of setbacks, I'm proud of you for at least sticking in the game.

George Bernard Shaw said, "When I was young, I observed that nine out of ten things I did were failures. So I did ten times more work."[153] If it takes you ten times the work effort to hit your goal, then that's where you're at. Rejoice! But we should be willing to do the work, and we should expect to get the results. If we can learn to be satisfied with *results food* over *activity food*, then we will earn the right to dine with kings and queens.

KEY POINTS

1. When you develop an appetite for *results food* over *activity food*, you'll have a much bigger feast to enjoy at life's banquet.

2. Get moving. Don't let yourself off the hook. I wouldn't pick up my '38 Donzi fishing boat until I hit my goal. Select a reward for nailing your goal, but don't indulge in the reward until you've crossed the finish line.

3. Never lower the bar on yourself. If you said you would sell $10,000 this month of your product and you sell $9,999, you have *not* hit your goal. Don't kid yourself.

4. You have to face reality in order to fix what isn't working in your life. Identify a problem and take action to fix it.

5. Decide what your BHAGs are (your Big Hairy Audacious Goals) and focus on them. If everything is a priority, then nothing is a priority.

6. Create a culture of positive peer pressure. As Tony Robbins

says, "We rise to the level of expectations of our peer group."[154]

7. Excuses are useless. It didn't matter that it was hard for me to soften my rough edges; it was necessary. Edward R. Murrow said, "Difficulty is the excuse history never accepts."[155]

ALL WARRIORS HAVE
WOUNDS TO BE MENDED

Courage doesn't always roar. Sometimes courage is the quiet voice at the end of the day saying, "I will try again tomorrow."[156]

—Mary Anne Radmacher

A t home, my younger boys love to play with their G.I. Joe action figures (and so do I). It's no big surprise that every once in a while, those little toys take a beating! Some of the soldiers face some pretty stiff opposition from the enemy and come back from the "front lines" with an arm or a leg knocked off.

It has become a fun little ritual that my boys will come find me and show me what's happened to these brave soldiers. I reassure them that these soldiers will be as good as new and that we will get them into G.I. Joe Hospital so they can be tended to. Now, just so you know, G.I. Joe Hospital is one of the finest battlefield triage units around for pint-sized plastic warriors. We've got the most advanced science and technology (Krazy Glue and pliers, and Gorilla Glue for severe injuries) and a luxurious recovery spa (the desk in my office).

After a day of fierce combat among the toys, my boys will run up and ask, "Dad, is there any room left in the hospital? Duke really bought it on this trip out!"

And I will grimly shake my head and say, "Boys, I'm not sure. I thought all the beds were filled up." Then after a minute, I let them off the hook and say, "I just checked with the medic. We can get Duke into surgery tonight. He'll be as good as new in the morning." Of course, I get big smiles and hugs for this!

These little toys don't face any real battles, but you and I do. Anyone who stands for something can expect to eventually fight in some way: We fight by saying no to something that is wrong, we fight to try again when we face a setback, we fight with words in a courtroom, and we might even fight against evil by shouldering a rifle on the battlefield. And when we fight, we can expect to take some punches.

With enough time, our minds and hearts will start to show the scars of the battle. In a way, each of us needs a G.I. Joe Hospital to mend his own wounds. The wounds are different for each of us: They can be the way a little part of one's heart is broken, or how one has a tough time trusting people again. Our wounds can be the feeling of fear from a terrible situation that we've faced in the past, the memory of which we can't seem to shake. Sometimes our wounds are physical, for the world to see on our bodies; sometimes our wounds are spiritual, for the world to see in our eyes.

> *Sometimes our wounds are physical, for the world to see on our bodies; sometimes our wounds are spiritual, for the world to see in our eyes.*

Here's what I know for sure: Everyone is wounded in some way, and everyone needs healing in some way. I believe true healing comes from God alone. The only way to realize our dreams is to decide to move past the hurt, be healed, and try again until we win.

All Great Leaders Face a Desert Experience

Never forget that life can only be nobly inspired and rightly lived if you take it bravely and gallantly, as a splendid adventure in which you are setting out into an unknown country, to meet many a joy, to find many a comrade, to win and lose many a battle.[157]

—Annie Besant

Chris Brady, best-selling author and close friend, talks about the fact that all great leaders have a "desert experience," where they go through a time of failure before reaching their goal. Of course, Chris is referring to the story of Moses and the Jewish people wandering the desert for forty years before reaching the Promised Land. Many great people face a similar experience, where success evaporates for a season. They lose much of what they had built, and from the outside, everything seems hopeless. But inside, they are growing and changing. They are mending their broken hearts and learning from their mistakes. They have been humbled, but they resolve to come back better and stronger than ever.

When we are striving for success in any area of life, each of us is going to face failure. It's not a matter of *if* we are going to face failure — it's a matter of *when* and *how much*. Don't be too surprised when it happens! It's all part of our journey. We shouldn't visualize failure and start expecting it. We should simply be aware that this is normal for everyone, so we don't get too down on ourselves when it occurs.

Life is a little like the changing of the seasons. We go through the spring, where opportunities emerge; we go through summer, with a lot of fun and excitement; we go through fall, where we enjoy the harvest and reap the reward of all our hard work; and then we face a winter. It's the same for everyone. In fact, when you read the stories of the most successful people on earth, you'll find that every one of them went through really tough times on the way to the top. Let's take a look at one guy who is known around the world and who, at what looked like the height of his success, faced what could have been a crushing setback.

From Founder to Fired and Back Again

Woz and I started Apple in my parents' garage when I was twenty. We worked hard, and in ten years Apple had grown from just the two of us in a garage into a $2 billion company with over 4,000 employees. We had just released our finest creation—the Macintosh—a year earlier, and I had just turned thirty. And then I got fired.[158]

—Steve Jobs

Steve Jobs (who, sadly, passed away during the time of this writing) had built one of the most successful companies on earth: Apple Inc. In the summer of 2011, Apple surpassed Exxon to momentarily become the highest valued company in America. It also surpassed Microsoft in market capitalization, becoming the world's most valuable tech company. And its founder Steve Jobs was a visionary CEO who didn't just create new *products*—he created new product *categories*.[159]

Steve Jobs, along with his business partner Steve Wozniak, famously invented one of the first personal computers the Apple with the little company the two had originally launched in their garage in 1976. Jobs was totally dedicated to creating the most amazing computers the world had ever seen. He knew his company was growing faster in some ways than he was, and he knew he needed a good corporate guy to handle the big operation.[160]

Jobs would eventually hire a guy named John Sculley, then president of Pepsi, to become the CEO of Apple Computers. Their working relationship was pretty good at the beginning. But by 1985, the company was having a tough time responding to a slow market. People were not buying as many computers as Apple had hoped. And Sculley had a hard time with Jobs's management style.[161]

Jobs was a great visionary, but a bit of a loose cannon. He had a temper, a tough time listening to anyone else's ideas, and (some say) a huge ego. Most people in his situation would struggle not to be arrogant: Jobs was worth a $1 million by the age of twenty-three, $10 million by the age of twenty-four, and $100 million by the age of twenty-five. And his overbearing and erratic style was making him difficult to work with. In time, Sculley and Jobs had a falling-out, and by 1985, Jobs faced a situation he could never have imagined: He was forced out of Apple by the guy he had hired.[162]

For Steve Jobs, it was a really humiliating public defeat. The company he had built, his baby, had been ripped away from him. In his now-famous commencement address to Stanford University in 2005, Jobs recounted what the experience had taught him:

> I really didn't know what to do for a few months. I was a very public failure, and I even thought about running away from the valley. But something slowly began to dawn on me—I still loved what I did. I had been rejected, but I was still in love. And so I decided to start over. I didn't see it then, but it turned out that getting fired from Apple was the best thing that could have ever happened to me. The heaviness of being successful was replaced by the lightness of being a beginner again, less sure about everything. It freed me to enter one of the most creative periods of my life.[163]

What happened next would literally transform the music, movie, phone, and personal computer industry. Jobs realized he loved technology, so he started another computer company called NeXT.[164]

Also, in 1986, Jobs bought a little computer graphics division from George Lucas, creator of the *Star Wars* movies.[165] Lucas called the division the Graphics Group. This name was later dropped, and the company now operates under a name you might recognize: Pixar. Pixar is now the most celebrated computer animation movie studio, having created twelve movies including *Toy Story* and *Cars*, and winning twenty-six Academy Awards in the process. When Pixar stock went public, Jobs became an instant billionaire.[166]

After Steve Jobs left Apple in 1985, the culture had started to change. You see, Jobs was a passionate, idealistic visionary, not a toe-the-line corporate guy. Jobs hired people who passionately loved Apple and loved creating world-class products. He wanted to change the world! When Jobs left Apple Inc., the heart of the company left with him. Over the next twelve years, as sales and stock declined, John Sculley was eventually forced to resign as CEO of Apple in 1993. Apple was orphaned of strong leadership for the time being.[167]

The interim leadership team was stuck. They realized they needed a new operating system, something that could carry them into the next century and help them compete in the marketplace. After a lot of searching, they found a computer technology company that had the exact operating system that would help them rebound. The irony was that the company and system they bought was NeXT, and the owner was Steve Jobs. After twelve years of wandering the proverbial desert, Jobs was returning to Apple.[168]

In 1996, Steve Jobs sold NeXT to Apple and was named interim CEO in 1997. When he returned to run the show at Apple, he was a wiser and more seasoned leader. His willpower was so strong that any obstacles his team imagined were removed by the force of his vision.[169]

In the following fifteen years, Jobs literally transformed the music industry by creating legal downloads at ninety-nine cents each through iTunes and the world's most popular music MP3 player the iPod. He took over the smartphone market that RIM created with its BlackBerry and crushed his previous rival with his user-friendly iPhone. And the iPad has basically created the tablet market all by itself, with every other competitor now playing catch-up.[170]

A desert experience has value only if we learn and grow from it. Although we may lose our way or lose sight of the path from time to time, we must not lose our vision of where we want to go. For Jobs, it had been a humbling experience to have been cast out of the empire he had built. The next two companies (NeXT and Pixar) didn't have the same fast-growth success as Apple did; they really struggled in their early years. All these experiences changed Jobs. When he returned home to Apple, he was more generous with sharing ideas and listening. He had become more collaborative. And all of this helped make him the legendary and unforgettable CEO who revolutionized four industries![171]

What Lessons Does Defeat Teach?

It is defeat that turns bone to flint, and gristle to muscle, and makes people invincible, and formed those heroic natures that are now in ascendancy in the world. Do not, then, be afraid of defeat. You are never so near to victory as when defeated in a good cause.[172]

—Henry Ward Beecher

Laurie Woodward likes to say, "The lesson continues until the lesson is learned." All of us are going to face lessons in our lives, and usually those lessons are wrapped up inside a gift box labeled "defeat." I've had some decent success in my life, and some huge setbacks. One of the things I've noticed is that I learn a lot more from defeat than from victory. When a person wins, he is usually too busy patting himself on the back and wallowing in pride to notice the real reasons he succeeded. But when one falls flat on his face, he stops and thinks about how to avoid repeating his mistakes.

One of the most upsetting moments in my life came from the end of my days playing football. I loved football and was regularly good enough to make the team. But while I was in high school, I had transferred back and forth between two schools. My mom had fought to keep me in the parochial school, but the annual tuition was too much for a single mom to cover every year. As I explained before, she was forced to transfer me back into the public school system.

Transferring schools created a couple of problems for me, and one of them was that I was ineligible to play football for a year. So going back to the public school system that year was a huge letdown for several reasons, one of which was having to watch the games from the sidelines.

While I was waiting for the next year to arrive, along with my opportunity to play again, I began a really advanced training program to help me get into competitive shape: I started drinking a lot and lying around. You should have seen my one-pack, not a six-pack, by the end of that summer. I was hardly a force to be reckoned with.

When I showed up that first day of tryouts, I discovered that the coach used a very popular, and very effective, technique to weed out the weak: He made us run. We ran the field, we ran the track, and then we ran up the bleachers. And we ran down the bleachers. And then he made us run up the bleachers once again to really make sure we got the point. And my finely-tuned body reacted as you might expect: I puked my guts out. I took a good look at the other guys competing for a spot on the team. It was obvious to me they were in better shape than I was. They had kept up their fitness routines, they had their heads in the game, and they flat out deserved it more than I did. So I walked off the field, utterly disgusted with myself, and quit football for good.

It's fair to say I wasn't going to ever make it to the NFL, but I was probably good enough to play in a small college. However, I was so consumed with my negative feelings and being down on myself that I threw in the towel and quit. I quit one of the things I loved the most, which had made me feel proud of myself in the past. And to "celebrate" my quitting, I walked over to my buddy's house and drank until I passed out.

I didn't want to feel the pain of quitting. I wanted to stop thinking about how badly it hurt to lose my love, the game of football, and my dream of playing. I wanted to stop thinking about how I'd let myself down. I drank to forget and to punish myself.

This kind of pain can dig deep into you. It can really leave some scars. It's up to each of us to decide how we use pain: Do we let it beat us down, or do we let it build us up? L. Thomas Holdcroft says, "Life is a grindstone. Whether it grinds us down or polishes us up depends on us."[173]

> *Life is a grindstone. Whether it grinds us down or polishes us up depends on us.*
> *— L. Thomas Holdcroft*

In my case, as time went on, my mind would drift back to football, and I would wonder what would have happened if I had not quit. Quitting had caused me such unbelievable pain, although I didn't know it at the time. And that is the point of this story: I decided that I would never ever quit again. Quitting just hurts too much.

Because of that, when it came time to build my leadership business, quitting on myself was off the table. I had walked down that road before, and I realized that no man could hurt Tim Marks as badly as he could hurt himself. My defeat was completely self-inflicted, and because of that lesson, I had a lot of motivation to *not* make the same mistake again. I resolved I would never quit, no matter what. That gave me a lot of strength when times were tough in the beginning. It's probably one of the biggest reasons I am where I am today: I will never ever quit on myself and my dreams again. The lesson I learned from quitting football is that the pain of regret is greater than the pain of defeat.

Character Is Formed from Great Difficulty

Character cannot be developed in ease and quiet. Only through experiences of trial and suffering can the soul be strengthened, vision cleared, ambition inspired and success achieved.[174]

—Helen Keller

The best guitarists have calloused fingertips. You can always spot a beginner because he has soft skin; experienced guitarists have calloused skin. Their skin has become tough and resistant because they have repeatedly gone through the discomfort of playing even when their fingers were sore. It hurt them to get to that point, but now they don't feel the pain anymore. This allows them to concentrate on playing great music. In fact, they wouldn't be able to play the fast passages and guitar licks without that tough skin.

Just as a great musician has to develop thick skin, so does everyone who wants to win. Whenever you see someone or something that has stood the test of time—whether it is a building, a monument, an oak tree, or a leader—you know it because that person or thing has faced hardship and has been forced to toughen up.

A great business leader I work with says that the best musical instruments are formed from trees that have the tightest grain. That type of grain is found only in trees that have faced hardship, where the winds never stopped blowing and the tree had to fight to force its roots down into the earth, pushing against rocky terrain and competing against other tree roots. Sometimes those trees don't get a lot of rain and sunshine. The trees become battle-hardened, and the wood they produce is the toughest and the best.

We grow strong when we face the winds that blow in our lives. Just as our muscles grow strong when we have to fight to lift weights, our spirit is forced to toughen up when we face our own personal storms. Storms come in different ways. We might lose a loved one to cancer. We might be injured and have to learn to walk again. We might get laid off from our jobs and lose our homes. Our spouses may walk out on us and our kids. We might have major setbacks in business. We might lose our faith and wonder if we will ever get it back. There are thousands and thousands of different kinds of storms that we will face at some point in our lives.

Here's what I've learned about success: Tough times help to toughen us up. Every storm is a chance to learn and grow and change. Romans 5:3–4 (ESV) says, "Not only that, but we rejoice in our sufferings, knowing that suffering produces endurance, and endurance produces character, and character produces hope." Whether or not you are a believer, I think everyone can learn

> *Tough times help to toughen us up.*

from the wisdom in those words.

If We Aren't Humble, We Will *Be* Humbled

For everyone who exalts himself will be humbled, and he who humbles himself will be exalted.

—Luke 14:11 (ESV)

Defeat can be a blessing. Many times it is. Defeat forces us to face reality and admit our weaknesses. If we are in the process of becoming a leader, defeat will prepare us for that responsibility. It's better to make a mistake leading a small group of people and improve yourself then, rather than *not* learn the lesson and make that same mistake when you are leading a large group of people.

Maybe we are harsh with people, as I was and sometimes still have to guard against. Maybe we are disorganized. Maybe we are moody or unpleasant to be around. Maybe we are negative. Whatever we need to improve on, defeat usually has a way of pointing out our *area of opportunity*. As Tommy Newbury says, "We often don't realize it, but we frequently come face-to-face with the exact obstacle we need at just the right time to sharpen us where we need it the most."[175] Hopefully, a person can swallow his pride, admit he needs to grow in a certain area, and say, "I need to overcome this weakness."

One area of character that defeat will really help us manage is that of pride and arrogance. If we aren't humble, we will *be* humbled—count on it! I know when I started having fast success in building my leadership business that I made the mistake of reading my press clippings. I listened to those who were praising me and cheering for me, and I started to get a big puffed-up chest, thinking I was all that and a bag of chips. Well, God corrected me on that one pretty quickly by causing my business to slow down until I faced my arrogance. In fact, any time my pride gets out of hand, he sends me a gentle little reminder to knock me back into place.

I'm amazed at how we struggle with pride and arrogance because, most of the time, we look pretty goofy to the people around us. It might do us some good to stop trying to look good all the time and just come down to earth. C. J. Mahaney, author of *Humility: True Greatness*, suggests one way to manage pride:

> First, play golf as much as possible. Yep, golf. In my athletic experience, I don't think there's a more difficult or humbling sport. Rather, humiliating—because if you play at all, you know all about those shots that result in laughter from your partners and humiliation for you. No one escapes them.[176]

I think we could all benefit by loosening up and allowing ourselves to look silly more often.

Orrin Woodward says we should value excellence over ego. I couldn't agree more. Whenever ego flares up, profits in business eventually go down. Just ask Jim Collins, author of *How the Mighty Fall*. He studied dozens of companies that had made it big, only to crash and burn badly. Jim started to notice an amazing pattern. In fact, he whittled the path from success to failure down to five key stages. He calls them the Five Stages of Decline. Guess what Stage One is. It's "Hubris born of success."[177]

Before Jim Collins noticed it, thousands of years ago, the Lord said in Proverbs 16:18 (ESV), "Pride goes before destruction, and a haughty spirit before a fall." I suppose when something is called a *principle*, it's because it's *always* true. So many politicians and movie stars become arrogant when they make it big.

> *Being humble doesn't mean you think less of yourself – it means you think of yourself less.*

Maybe they think they are above the rules. Maybe they think they can simply go around having affairs and breaking the law and that the natural laws of right and wrong somehow don't apply to them anymore. Well, I've learned in life that if we aren't humble, we will

176

be humbled. Charles Spurgeon, "the Prince of Preachers," said, "The Christian is in his best state when he is poor in self and rich in Christ."[178] Being humble doesn't mean you *think less of yourself*—it means you *think of yourself less*.

HEAL THY WOUNDED HEART

Things don't go wrong and break your heart so you can become bitter and give up. They happen to break you down and build you up so you can be all that you were intended to be.[179]

—Samuel Johnson

Defeat can poison one's spirit. Every individual looks for answers and wonders what went wrong when one comes in second place or last. Sometimes one's spirit can be poisoned against another person. Maybe the other individual hurt you in some way, perhaps through a betrayal. You might blame that person and say to yourself, "You let me down! I would have been successful if it weren't for you!" That is a dangerous thought that I would encourage you to avoid.

I've learned in my life that some people might lie to you. Some people might steal from you. Some people might attack you unfairly and accuse you of things you never did. Some people might question your morals and values and say you are a bad person. Some people might make a promise and say, "You can count on me," and then not keep their word. And all of this can hurt.

When we are hurt, beaten down, and feel betrayed by the people we love, how do we react? Do we become bitter or better? Do we allow angry feelings to fester and grow? Do we become so bitter we start to change how we think of and feel toward people? Sadly, this has happened to many folks with whom I have worked over the years.

177

In fact, if we've been hurt badly enough, we might start to look at all people a little differently. We might look at people and remember the pain we've gone through, and we might decide, "People are liars. You can't trust them!" This might appear to be true to some people. If we grow up in a tough neighborhood with a lot of crime and gang violence, as did my great friend Bill Lewis — and Bill has overcome those circumstances to become a very successful business owner — our situation can change the way we look at people. We may have seen so much of the bad stuff that it becomes tough for us to believe there is any good at all.

A wise man once said, "Being angry towards other people and wanting revenge on them is like drinking poison and expecting the other person to die." Anger and bitterness just eat at our guts like acid. They burn big holes through our hearts and leave us empty inside.

> *Anger and bitterness just eat at our guts like acid. They burn big holes through our hearts and leave us empty inside.*

Andy Andrews, famed comedian, inspirational speaker and *New York Times* best-selling author of *The Traveler's Gift*, says this about anger:

> We need to forgive others. That doesn't mean that the person who wronged you shouldn't be held accountable for his actions. Forgiveness isn't a tool to let the *other* guy off the hook; it's a tool to let *you* off the hook. It's a tool that allows you to let go of the anger in your heart.

> *Forgiveness isn't a tool to let the other guy off the hook; it's a tool to let you off the hook. It's a tool that allows you to let go of the anger in your heart.*
> *— Andy Andrews*

I would even say it goes deeper than that. A *tool* just helps you do a job better. Without forgiveness, you can't really do the *job* of loving people completely. We can't give what we don't have. If we have bitterness in our hearts, that's all we have to offer others, at least at some level.

I have worked with a lot of wounded warriors – business leaders who have faced setbacks and had their hearts broken. Fortunately, I've been one as well. I say *fortunately* since I feel that I'm a better husband, father, leader, and mentor because of it. I've gone through my own suffering and have developed some perspective to help others through theirs. One of the biggest hurdles for a wounded warrior is letting go of the baggage, the pain of the event he went through. That is much easier said than done. For me, it was a combination of prayer, being mentored, listening to a lot of CDs, and reading a lot of books.

Eileen Caddy said:

> Dwell not on the past. Use it to illustrate a point, and then leave it behind. Nothing really matters except what you do now in this instant of time. From this moment onwards you can be an entirely different person, filled with love and understanding, ready with an outstretched hand, uplifted and positive in every thought and deed.[180]

There is some wisdom in that perspective.

Think about the idea of getting squeezed or put in a position where you're under a lot of pressure. Now, think about squeezing an orange. When you do that, what comes out of the orange? If you guessed orange juice, you would be right. Now, imagine yourself in a pressure situation. When you get squeezed, what comes out of you? Is it bitterness, hostility, anger, rudeness, selfishness, or something else? Our true nature gets revealed when the chips are down. It's easy to fake being a nice guy when times are easy; we find out what we are really made of when times are tough. When we are squeezed by life, is it anger that comes out, or acceptance? Is it grief or grace? Is it frustration or forgiveness? I get to see my true heart in action when I'm under pressure.

My Family Secret

I n preparing this book, I seriously debated whether to include this next story. It has never been revealed publicly and, as this book was nearing completion, only a few trusted confidants knew of it. As you are now reading these words, we will have completed all of the DNA testing to officially confirm what I am about to share with you.

This story starts at a time around 2001, when I was five months into a six-month sprint to create a million-dollar annual income and achieve a pretty significant business victory. I was working very hard and doing a lot of large business presentations. I found myself up in Grand Blanc, Michigan, one night; as usual, I was shaking a lot of hands and saying "Hi" to a lot of people. I had gotten into the friendly habit of saying, "Hey, buddy" or "Hey, brother" when I met folks. Well, I said, "Hey, how are you doing, brother?" to a guy at the meeting, and he looked totally stunned. Later, I would learn why.

You see, it turns out we really are brothers – actual, real-life, biological brothers! When I had spoken to him at the meeting and said, "Hey…brother" as a friendly greeting, he thought it was my way of telling him I knew the secret. I suppose that he went home that night and called his father to tell him, and that set things into motion.

A little while later, I got a phone call from a guy I remembered from my past. He invited me for coffee. The name rang a bell: The guy phoning me was my mom's old high-school boyfriend, Clyde. I hadn't seen him in years, and at that time, it had been nine years since my mom had passed away. I figured maybe he was calling to reminisce about my mom or to return some stuff of hers to me.

We met at his house—this old boyfriend of my mom's and me. For some reason, it was a little awkward. He cleared his throat and dropped a bomb on me.

"Tim, before your mom died, she made me promise that I would take our secret to the grave with me. I've kept my word till now, but I've got a bad back as I'm getting older, and I thought you should know what I'm going to tell you in case you have any health concerns that might be hereditary."

I was really confused; I didn't understand what he was trying to say to me.

"You see, Tim, your mom and dad went through some tough times in their marriage. Because we had been friends in high school, your mom felt comfortable talking to me about the stuff she was going through. It was during one of those rough patches that your mom and I met one night at a ski hill. We got to talking, and then we started kissing. Then one thing led to another, and nine months later, you were born."

I couldn't speak. I wanted to deny it, but in that moment, I absolutely knew he was telling the truth. I looked at this guy's face, and it was like looking in a mirror. There was no doubt in my mind that I was sitting across the table from my biological father. It didn't matter that I didn't want it to be real. We can deny something all day long, and that will not change the fact that it is true.

He saw the look on my face and started to stammer. "Maybe I shouldn't have done this," he began.

I said angrily, "Well, you did." And I just got up. "I don't know what to think about all this," I told him and then walked out.

I drove home with a big knot in my gut. I walked in through the door, found Amy, and told her the whole story. I was numb, trying to mentally process what this meant about me and my kids and my family. It meant my brother was my half-brother, and half of my cousins, aunts, uncles, and grandparents *weren't* actually my family. And it meant that somewhere, there was a whole other group of people whom I really didn't know that *were* my family. Every family reunion I had ever been to on my dad's side of the family was a farce. I had only really ever met half of my real family—the people on my mother's side.

At least it explained why I was the only guy on my dad's side who tanned. It turns out that my real great-grandfather was one-quarter Cherokee Indian. I learned some other interesting family history over time: My grandfather was the biggest baby born in Missouri at the time at sixteen pounds and fourteen ounces, and my great-grandmother was the illegitimate child of the Vanderbilt family – so I guess I have entrepreneurial blood in my veins.

I called Orrin and went to his house. We prayed. I thank God for that man being my friend and mentor and being there for me in that moment. I was so overwhelmed I started thinking, "What if my mom had had an abortion in order to hide what she had done? Neither I nor my kids would exist." I praise God that she decided to keep me.

I didn't have a choice about the fact that I was born out of wedlock, that I was the result of one guy's affair with a married woman, and that I was a bastard child because of it.

Orrin said, "Tim, it doesn't matter who your earthly father is. You know who your Heavenly Father is."

Some of the people reading this might have gone through a similar situation, or a situation that similarly rocked them to the core. I was in the middle of the biggest business sprint of my life, and I'll be honest, this was like a punch in the gut. It left me winded and gasping for air. I was a little overwhelmed by it. But I chose to give thanks for what I had. I gave thanks for my mom's decision to keep me, for the blessing of Amy and my kids in my life, for the blessing of Orrin's counsel, and for my Heavenly Father who loves me. His grace helped heal my heart so I could move on and, hopefully, be a blessing in the lives of others.

All of us are going to face moments that make us feel as though our whole world has been rocked. We can choose to give in to anger, sadness, and pain; or we can choose to pray, read, and reach out for help from a trusted friend or mentor. To win in life, we have to learn to heal our hearts so we can accept the blessing that is probably right around the corner. Honestly, I've witnessed how some people encounter struggles or events that seem to me to be way less significant, and yet they get totally paralyzed by little matters. It's not *what* happens to you that matters as much as *how* you respond.

> *It's not* what *happens to you that matters as much as* how *you respond.*

PERSEVERE AND RISE AGAIN

The most essential factor is persistence—the determination never to allow your energy or enthusiasm to be dampened by the discouragement that must inevitably come.[181]

—James Whitcomb

Everyone's life is like a roller coaster: You go up, then you go down, and then you go up again. Every person faces really good times and then really tough times. The bigger the highs, the lower the lows will be. And like many people, I have faced some pretty low lows and some pretty high highs, and I praise God for both.

When I was building my real estate empire (By now, you already know that I was the farthest thing from Donald Trump you could imagine.), I had hired a property manager to take care of many of the details of running my daily operations. This was a great idea on paper. Sometimes, an idea that looks great in the planning stages doesn't execute as well as you had hoped. When the idea jumps off the blueprint into real life, some other factors come into play. Specifically, if you hire someone to oversee your business, you should make sure you hire someone you can trust. This is a lesson I learned in a very painful way.

As I was shifting my focus from my real estate business to my leadership business, I finally made the decision to quit my job as an engineer so I could focus on building my business full-time. To raise some cash, I sold three of my rental houses and figured that would buy me a couple of months. Because I no longer had a salary, I was living off the income from my rental properties.

Then the proverbial chicken hit the fan. I discovered that twenty of my thirty-plus rental properties were empty. My property manager had apparently cooked the books. She had been in cahoots with the repair guy. They had dreamed up a scheme to skim as much cash out of my rental company as possible by posting fake repair claims and having the repair guy swing by to fix the problems. The issue was that there were no problems (or at least, not the problems for which I was paying). The repair guy would submit an invoice for work and materials, and my property manager would cut him a check. It turned out that the repairman was her boyfriend.

I was devastated when I discovered this. Everything I had worked to build was on a foundation of sand. The rental income I was expecting simply evaporated. To add insult to injury, after I figured it out, the property manager quit on me and then turned around and sued me! Words can't describe how I felt.

My lawyer simply advised me to file for bankruptcy, settle with my property manager, and wash my hands of it. He felt that trying to sue her in return was pointless; she had spent all the cash she had stolen from me, and she had nothing with which to repay me. My lawyer found out that I wasn't the first person who had fallen prey to her scheme. I decided to settle out of court; I cut her a check and then just walked away.

I had owned over thirty rental houses, each valued from $25,000 to $70,000, plus my own house. In total, I had over $1.3 million in debt hanging around my neck. Every month I was going backward $15,000 with all the mortgages, second mortgages, repair bills, and credit lines. To describe my situation as desperate would be a pretty big understatement. Our little rowboat hadn't just sprung a financial leak, it had hit an iceberg and was sinking like the *Titanic*.

I did anything I could to keep our noses above water. Anytime a credit card application arrived in the mail, I filled it out and returned it as fast as I could. When my own credit rating got so bad, I would get a credit card in Amy's name out of desperation. I would sign up for four or five at a time just to stay afloat. And I was doing everything I could to protect Amy and the kids from knowing what was going on.

One of the most humiliating moments came when Amy was standing at the grocery checkout line and tried to use a credit card to buy food. It was declined. She tried another card with the same result. She tried every account we had and ended up having to put some of the food back, which was obviously very humiliating. She had to put forty dollars on one card and sixty dollars on another just to come home with something to eat. She called me on the phone to tell me about this, and I could hear the fear in her voice.

I felt crushed inside; I couldn't even afford to buy groceries for my wife and kids. I remember just sitting in my basement and weeping — openly sobbing, with tears rolling down my cheeks, my head in my hands, and praying to God not just to get me out of this mess, but to get me through and far beyond it. We were on the verge of losing everything. I was doing everything I could to shield my family from what was happening, and I felt that I was failing miserably. It was one of the darkest times of my life.

I would stay in my bleak basement time and again, sitting at my dingy old desk. I would make phone calls to Western Union to have money wired from a credit card in order to pay a mortgage. Amy would call down and ask me what I was doing, and I would tell her, "It's nothing, honey. It's just real estate stuff." She was so trusting of me that she never asked further. And I would continue to weep and to pray.

To this day, the memory of that basement haunts me. Beside my dingy old desk, where I would sit in the corner and make calls to Western Union, there had been an old sump pump, and it would turn on every once in a while. It would whine and gurgle, and the dank water would be pushed out. I would time my phone calls to make them between pump cycles. I'll never forget that sound as long as I live. If I'm ever in a basement and hear that sound, my stomach turns; it instantly takes my mind back to those dark times and dark feelings. I never want to hear that sound again.

People ask me, "How did you do it?" The better question to ask me is, "*Why* did I do it?" I knew I had to build my leadership business because my finances were dwindling fast. All this real estate stuff started happening even before I received the shocking news about my

185

family. Maybe other people would have given up if they had faced a similar situation. I suppose I could have rolled over and thrown in the towel too, but I wasn't going to quit on Amy and the kids. I've learned that if you have a big-enough *why*, you can bear any *how*.

Norman Vincent Peale said, "Any fact facing us is not as important as our attitude toward it, for that determines our success or failure. The way you think about a fact may defeat you before you ever do anything about it. You are overcome by the fact because you think you are."[182] We have to decide to ignore the facts and concentrate on putting one foot in front of the other, and eventually, success will come our way.

From Courtroom Drama to Courtroom Writer

When most people hear the word *no*, they run for cover. If we want to win at anything, we have to be prepared to face some setbacks and some defeats. Each of us has to develop a thicker skin so when those rejections eventually come, they will feel, as Orrin Woodward says, like "spitballs off of a battleship." Overnight success takes years. Most people fail or fall into mediocrity because of a lack of *stick-to-it-iveness*. (And to all the English professors out there, yes, it is a real word.)

One famous example of a guy who wouldn't give up at the first sign of rejection is a guy named John. John was a smart kid who grew up in Mississippi in the 1970s, born to two parents who had no formal education. Despite this, his mother would always encourage him to read so that he could be the first person in their family to get a college degree.[183]

He drifted from one school to the next, attending three separate colleges before finally graduating with a degree in law. He started a modest law practice in Mississippi and had some success. In time, he realized he didn't feel too challenged with his practice, so he successfully ran for and won a seat in the House of Representatives in

1983. His schedule started to get pretty busy as he juggled his work as a public servant and being a tireless advocate of the people.[184]

One day in court, he happened to overhear the testimony of another trial going on next door. A twelve-year-old girl was on the stand and was telling the jury the story of how she had been assaulted. John couldn't stop thinking about that girl; he imagined how he would feel if he had been the girl's father. Would he want to have revenge on the criminal? He couldn't get this question out of his head. He went home and started putting his thoughts down on paper.[185]

As time went on, he started to sketch out a fictional tale of just such a situation, with a vigilante father in his story avenging his daughter's attack. John became consumed with telling the story of this girl and her family. His passion grew, and he resolved to write a book.[186]

The first obstacle he faced was time. He was a busy guy! He was already looking at an overwhelming schedule, working eighty to ninety hours a week as he split his time between the state legislature and his law practice. How would he ever find the time to write? Most people would just give up on their dreams, or tell themselves they would get around to following their dreams later when they weren't as busy.[187]

But John was consumed with his dream of writing this book. He felt this was a story that had to be told. And so, John decided to wake up every day at 5:00 a.m. and write, and he did that for *three years in a row*. He had a simple goal: just write one page every day. The book slowly took shape. By 1988, he had finished his first book *A Time to Kill*.[188]

John Grisham proudly mailed his manuscript to a publishing house. He was excited to see his career as a writer take off! Soon after, he received his first rejection notice. So John did what any bullheaded Viking would do: He mailed it out again to another publishing house. Once again, it was the same story. He thought, "The third time's the charm, right?" Nope, he was rejected again. In fact, he had tried thirty times and gotten thirty rejections.[189]

Finally, someone accepted his manuscript — the same publisher who had discovered Stephen King. The publisher was so skeptical of John's book they printed only five thousand copies. It didn't sell. Desperate, John personally went from bookstore to bookstore and bought one thousand copies. He invested thousands of dollars of his own money to fill his car trunk with copies of his book, and he drove around trying to set up book-signing events to generate some buzz. The book was a total failure; no one was interested. John returned from his road trip with his tail between his legs and egg on his face.[190]

Imagine yourself in this same situation. What would you do? You've just spent every single day of the last three years pouring your heart into a dream, scratching out a few precious minutes each day while the rest of the world slept, only to receive dozens of rejections in the end. Imagine finally getting a lukewarm yes only to see your book fail after you had invested thousands and thousands of dollars of your own money. Most people would quit. Most people would give up. But John wasn't like most people.[191]

Do you know what John did? He decided to start writing a *second* book! The same drill, the same exhausting schedule, and this time with some extra baggage under his belt called *failure*. For his second time up to bat, John decided to write a story about a young lawyer who discovered that his law firm was in bed with the mob, that everyone at the firm was monitored round the clock, and that anyone who dared expose the secret ended up dead. That book was called *The Firm*.[192]

This time, John Grisham got a very different response. The response wasn't from a publishing house—it was from Paramount Pictures. They wanted to buy the rights to the book and turn it into a movie starring Tom Cruise. John got a check for $600,000, and *The Firm* ended up on the best-seller list for forty-seven weeks, eventually selling over seven million copies. Through talent, work ethic, and perseverance, John Grisham became one of the most successful authors in America, with eight of his books made into motion pictures. He had failed miserably, but he had the guts to try again. And because of that, he won big![193]

Resolve to Finish What You Start

All endeavor calls for the ability to tramp the last mile, shape the last plan, endure the last hour's toil. The fight-to-the-finish spirit is the one characteristic we must possess if we are to face the future as finishers.[194]

—Henry David Thoreau

It's great to persevere. It's great to keep soldiering on and trying hard to hit our goals. But when we're wounded in some way, it's pretty common to start limping. We might start limping mentally by giving in to doubt. Our self-talk might be in the toilet, and we might start putting ourselves down. We might be so mentally, physically, or spiritually exhausted that it takes all of our strength just to stand up again when we get knocked down.

Standing up again is a good starting point. But standing doesn't take you anywhere. Walking takes you somewhere. Moving in the direction of your goals takes you closer to them. You've got to be in motion. So, as proud of you as I am to hear about when you got knocked down and then got back up again, I still encourage you to not merely stand but to *run*. There is a huge difference between a *willingness* to accomplish your goal and an *eagerness* to accomplish your goal. For example, some people might be willing to read their Bibles in the

> *There is a huge difference between a* willingness *to accomplish your goal and an* eagerness *to accomplish your goal.*

morning. I am eager to read my Bible in the morning. Ask yourself, "Am I eager to accomplish my goal?"

For me, keeping my word is a big deal. When I say I'm going to do something, God willing, I do it. I believe my integrity rides on keeping my promises, no matter how tough it might be, or how tired or discouraged I might feel. Sometimes I've felt as if I don't have the power to lift the phone to my ear and make another business call. When I feel as if I've lost all of my earthly ability to go on, I am reminded of Philippians 4:13: "I can do all things through Christ who strengthens me" (New King James Version).

To *persevere* means to follow a course of action despite all setbacks and obstacles. That is the second-to-last stage it takes to get the gold medal. The final stage is to *finish*. Don't just trudge along toward the finish line—*sprint* toward it.

Determined to Win the Gold Medal

K*ároly Takács* might not be a name you recognize, but he is an amazing example of someone who finished what he started. He was a sergeant in the Hungarian army in 1936 and was a world-class pistol shooter. In fact, he was so good that he was preparing to go to Tokyo and compete in the 1940 Olympics. He was highly favored at that time to be a strong contender for the gold medal, and he had decided that he was not only going to compete, he was going to bring home the medal for Hungary.[195]

One day, during a routine training exercise, something horrible happened. Takács was holding a grenade in his right hand, and it exploded, blowing his hand off completely. It was a miracle he even survived. He lay for days in a hospital bed recovering; to his friends and family, it seemed that his dream of winning the gold medal in pistol shooting was dead forever.[196]

However, Takács was a fighter. He decided to "set his goals in concrete and his plans in sand," as best-selling author Chris Brady is fond of saying. His goal was to win the gold medal in pistol shooting. His plan had been to do it using his right hand. Lying in that hospital bed, Takács started to dream. He imagined stepping up and shooting a perfect score to claim the medal—using his left hand![197]

As soon as he was out of the hospital, he began training in secret.

190

He trained for months. He was driven to shock everyone with the power of his mind to overcome obstacles and accomplish his goal. He never revealed to anyone what he was doing. To Hungarians, the loss of this man's hand was like watching Michael Jordan lose a foot and be unable to jump to shoot another basketball, or watching Wayne Gretsky be unable to skate again. It was a crushing national blow.[198]

You can only imagine the reaction when he showed up in 1939 to the Hungarian national pistol shooting championship. Friends and competitors alike were stunned that this man, a hero, had come out to watch them play. They figured it was breaking his heart, and they ran over to pay their condolences for his injury and his loss to the sport.[199]

Takács just laughed! He said, "I didn't come here to watch you play — I came here to compete!" They were stunned. They were even more surprised at the end of the day when Takács walked off with the trophy, having won the entire contest using his left hand.[200]

> *I didn't come here to watch you play - I came here to compete!*
> *— Károly Takács*

Then, World War II broke out, and the Tokyo Olympics were canceled. The war dragged on, and it seemed as though Takács would never be able to fulfill his dream of winning the gold medal. But as Jean le Rond d'Alembert said, "The difficulties you meet will resolve themselves as you advance. Proceed, and light will dawn, and shine with increasing clearness on your path." Károly Takács was a living example of that idea. Despite all of his setbacks, he continued to train, hoping he would have a chance to fight and win.[201]

His chance came in 1944 with the London Olympics. After almost a decade of heartbreaking setbacks, Takács not only showed up to the Olympics, but his performance was so good he set a new world record for pistol shooting and took home the gold medal.[202]

This guy would have had every right to feel sorry for himself. That's the normal response for a lot of us! But he wouldn't give in to self-pity. He worked as hard as he could behind the scenes to prove to everyone what is possible when you set your mind to something. So the question for us is this: Have there been times in our lives when we have been injured yet could still shoot left-handed, but we chose not to? Károly Takács faced that question and made a courageous choice. Because of that, today in Hungary, Károly Takács is a national hero and an example to each of us that we can, and *should*, finish what we start.[203]

CONCLUSION

I don't measure a man's success by how high he climbs but how high he bounces when he hits bottom.[204]

—General George S. Patton

Everybody has his or her heart broken at some point and feels defeated inside and outside. Someone might have lost a client, or maybe a friendship. Some people might have lost a loved one, and some might have lost their faith. Every great success story has some sort of setback, where the hero is smashed up against the rocks, bleeding, and wondering how he or she will ever keep going. And then, the hero licks his wounds, stands up, and fights to win the gold medal. As Norman Vincent Peale said, "Stand up to your obstacles and do something about them. You will find that they haven't half the strength you think they have."[205] My story and your story have setbacks for sure, but if we keep these ideas in mind, our stories will have victories, too.

KEY POINTS

1. We need to remember that everyone faces challenges and setbacks. It is normal for each of us to go through tough times on the journey toward success.

2. We can always learn from our experiences, especially when we've faced defeat.

3. Every wounded warrior has to mend his or her heart, because it's tough to move on when you are carrying a lot of pain, sadness, or anger in your heart. We all need to forgive, grow, and let go.

4. Winners have stick-to-it-iveness. They don't give up. They might get knocked down seven times, but they get back up every time.

5. Finish strong. As Mater from the Pixar movie *Cars* says, "Git'er done."[206]

WORK HARD, PLAY HARD, AND LIVE ON PURPOSE

Three grand essentials to happiness in this life are something to do, something to love, and something to hope for.[207]
—Joseph Addison

In his wonderful book *The 7 Habits of Highly Effective People*, author Stephen Covey uses the example of "sharpening your saw." As the story goes, if you need to chop down a tree, you should spend some time sharpening your saw first; otherwise, you get worn out working and are less effective. The metaphor is a great way to approach how we should balance work and life. If we are always working and never take the time to take care of ourselves by sharpening our saws, we are going to burn out, and we won't be effective.[208]

So how do we take care of ourselves? Well, we certainly need to prioritize our health and fitness. We've got to exercise, eat well, and go to the doctor preventatively as well as when we are concerned something serious might be happening. We also need to have friendships that are rewarding and energizing; we have to go out and have some fun! St. Thomas Aquinas said, "Friendship is the source of the greatest pleasures, and without friends, even the most agreeable pursuits become tedious."[209]

Finally, as you are aware, I am a Christian, and I try to begin every day by reading my daily devotionals and praying. This is the most important time in my day, and it gives me incredible peace and renewal. Without my Lord, I am nothing.

So as we come to the close of the book, I want to share a few thoughts on things that will help sharpen the saw. Even Vikings need to rest and relax between battles!

HAVE FUN, MAKE MONEY

Create an environment that is fun and you create an environment that people want to be a part of.[210]

—Rich DiGirolamo

In our business organization, we have a motto: "Have fun, make money, and make a difference." You'll notice that "Have fun" comes first. We believe you should find joy in the journey! In fact, it's so important we have decided it's a priority in life. We define the eight categories of life under the heading of the "8 Fs" — which stand for *faith, family, finances, fitness, freedom, following, friends,* and *fun*. To have a successful life, you need success in all eight areas, which means you should have great friends, as well as a lot of fun!

One of the greatest joys of my life is that, having built a successful business, I get to hang out and have fun with some of the greatest people I've ever known. Joseph Addison said, "Friendship improves happiness and abates misery by doubling our joys and dividing our grief."[211] It's my hope for you, as you pursue your own goals and achieve success, that you are able to bring your friends along with you. It's no fun being rich and sitting by your

> *Friendship improves happiness and abates misery by doubling our joys and dividing our grief.*
> *— Joseph Addison*

pool alone. You want a bunch of buddies who are rich, retired, and looking to hang out and have fun with you!

Off-Roading in Baja

Chris Brady is one of my best friends in the world; he's like a brother to me. We've gotten our pilot's licenses together, we've gone snorkeling together, we've explored other countries together, and we have had so many fun adventures and enjoyed so many inside jokes that we just have a blast hanging out.

One time, Chris and I rented some dune buggies to race across the Baja desert in Mexico. We bought the best racing suits money could buy – shoes, gloves, the whole bit – everyone else: jeans. Man, did we stick out! Neither of us knew anything about the Baja Desert or the expensive purpose-built cars we were in, but we sure *looked* good! We started mouthing off to the trip leader that we were going to be at the front of the pack, and he just shrugged and said, "Sure, sure, everybody says that!" Well, he hadn't met two guys nearly as competitive as Chris and I. In fact, we were so focused on beating everybody that we kind of ignored the fact that our brakes had failed!

We were zooming down the mountain at one point, and over one side of the road was a three-hundred-foot drop. If we had gone over the side, that would have been the end of Chris and Tim! Well, we were having far too much fun for me to tell Chris that we might be facing certain death. I just did my best to slow down by downshifting, right up until we faced a big bank of dirt on one side of the road.

I just hit it at full speed, slid up a bit toward the three-hundred-foot cliff, yanked that wheel to the left as hard as I could, and kept on zooming down. Chris said, "Wow, that was pretty cool, but why didn't you use the brakes?"

I finally fessed up: "Well, Chris, we haven't had brakes for quite a while!"

You see, people who think that horsepower and safety go together are wildly misled. You are never going to have as much fun in life if

197

you always play it safe rather than choosing to flirt with danger a little. In fact, for those with a choleric/D personality—aggressive, goal-oriented people—their final words are often, "Hey guys, watch this!" right before they do something really dangerous or stupid!

> *You are never going to have as much fun in life if you always play it safe.*

So as we were nearing the final stretch, we were coming down a hill and were passing a Mexican drug rehab place. As you can imagine, their sewage system was not exactly world-class. So there was a big stream of stinky sewage just seeping across the road. It was like runny molasses, and we were headed right for it. Luckily, I was in the driver's seat, so I aimed my wheel for a rock and got my tire up and over the problem. Sadly, Chris did not fare as well.

There aren't any windows on dune buggies, and Chris was sitting in the passenger seat when the tire on his side hit the stream of yucky sewage head-on. It sprayed up like a geyser, splashing all over his helmet and suit. Man, it was gross! He started sputtering and yelling, "You got this all over me!" And we started laughing.

Not a hundred yards away, I spotted a big flowering bush. I gunned the engine and ran the buggy right through it! I hit it so hard that a big branch snapped right off, came through the cage, and basically smacked Chris right in the face! It was a lilac bush, so then Chris was covered in lilacs and smelled like perfume. I said, "There you go, partner!" I stank him up and then got him smelling good in twenty seconds!

You see, it's great to make a lot of money, but it's so much more rewarding to have friends to enjoy the victory with. In addition to that Baja trip, we have ten more stories just as fun! Being part of an elite group of leaders and getting to horse around and celebrate your hard work with fun times is a joy everyone should experience. You can have great friends and enjoy great times, having fun and celebrating your own victory, if you do the work to chase your dreams and achieve your goals.

The PPTP

E very year, a terrible injustice occurs off the waters of Southwest Florida. Thousands of tarpon migrate into our waters, unaware of the terrible danger that lies waiting for them. These friendly fish are minding their own business, bothering no one, and yet they are viciously attacked by sharks. The gentle tarpon have no natural defense against these thoughtless and violent predators, and nothing has been done to protect them – until now.

Unbeknownst to many people, I belong to a black-ops division of the federal government code-named the PPTP. This stands for *People Protecting the Tarpon Population*. This division is so black-ops that if you belong to the federal government, you've never even heard of us.[1]

In conjunction with the local law enforcement and the Coast Guard (although both the Coast Guard and the local law enforcement are utterly unaware of this), I have spearheaded our division of the PPTP and have labored diligently to protect the tarpon. Doing so usually involves recruiting up-and-coming leaders on my business team to come down to Florida for the day, where we head out to sea to do battle with the local hammerhead and bull sharks. As you know, I've purchased a new '38 Donzi fishing boat, which is the latest tool in our arsenal for protecting the tarpon.

A typical day for the PPTP involves chumming up the water with as much blood and guts as we can (because that's what attracts the sharks) and enjoying some great leadership camaraderie. It takes a little while for the chum to drift out far enough to attract the sharks, but when they get a scent of the blood, they are on top of us in a jiffy.

If you've ever seen the movie *Jaws*, our fishing adventures are similar to those depicted in that movie (minus the part where the shark sinks the boat and eats Quint, the captain). Just like in the movie, the fishing line quivers a little as the shark nibbles away at the bait, and you start to hear the *click click click* sound from the reel.[212] (The bait we use is usually something big. Most people catch something like a four-

---

1   For the government lawyers reading this, just go along with the joke!

foot barracuda and mount it on the wall. We just chop it up and use it as bait for the really big fish.)

As soon as we figure we've got a winner on the other end of the line, we yank that line with all we've got and set the hook in its mouth, and we're off to the races! These fish are *huge*; hammerheads can often get to be more than twelve feet long and weigh thousands of pounds. (Incidentally, the world-record tarpon and hammerhead shark were both caught minutes from my house.) These hammerheads are longer than your family sedan and weigh almost as much, and they have mouths full of razor-sharp teeth that could cut through almost anything. And when we set that hook, they aren't just dangerous— they're *angry*.

The PPTP has had its share of victories, losses, and even a few misadventures. One time, we had a shark on the line that we figured was a hammerhead. Hammerheads usually circle the boat and are even strong enough to drag the boat a little. He had circled the boat enough that the line actually got caught underneath the boat on the transducer. The transducer is an important piece of technology; it is excellent at its job of showing proper water depth and tracking groups of fish. It is also excellent at snagging your fishing line when you are fighting with an angry hammerhead!

So on the day this was happening, two of my friends and business leaders from Kansas were with me on the boat. It was a father-and-son team, and the younger of the two sons has a choleric personality, which means he applies the "ready, *fire*, aim!" method of thinking things through. Well, no sooner had I announced that the line must be snagged on the transducer than this young man stated matter-of-factly, "Well, I guess someone will need to go under the boat and take care of it."

There are moments in life when things happen so fast all you can do is stare with your mouth open. Before I could even react, this young man had taken his shirt off, jumped into the water, and gone under the boat!

Now, we figured that the hammerhead shark was about forty yards off the bow. However, a hungry hammerhead can swim forty yards in about two seconds, and even quicker if he is mad and hungry. And we had been chumming the water to get this shark looking for a meal! After a few moments, we started to get worried. It felt to us as though this young man had been down there a little too long. I imagined that if the hammerhead hadn't gotten him, maybe his hand was caught in the line under the boat! (Man, imagine how that would wreck the hydrodynamics of my boat, having to drag that guy around all over the place!)

Luckily, he popped out of the water a moment later, and we caught the hammerhead and disciplined him for the tarpon murders he had most likely committed. Whew! Protecting the tarpon can be dangerous work! It's nice to be able to get to spend the day on my fishing boat with my friends and enjoy some great fun and great adventures — even when those friends are a little crazy!

Black Boots vs. White Boots

A great pleasure I share with my best friends is our back-and-forth banter and our inside jokes. Those are some of the best glues for every long-standing friendship. However, there are times when we must set aside even the greatest of friendships and take a stand on an "important" issue. This is one of those times.

For the last few years, I have engaged in a very public and spirited campaign to advocate for the more *masculine* and *correct* choice when deciding what color of boots one should wear while riding motocross bikes. There seems to be some confusion over this issue throughout the larger business organization with which I associate, so I felt it was my responsibility to take this moment and put the *official* answer down in print. For those people in my organization, I want to deeply apologize for any misinformation to which you have been exposed.

Some people think (quite incorrectly, I must say) that it's somehow cool to wear white motorcycle boots. Perhaps this thinking stems from discovering an Evel Knievel toy doll from 1976 with white boots and wrongly believing that this sets a precedent for all men to follow thereafter. (I can only assume that Evel and others were persuaded by the white-cow industry!) Luckily, people get wiser as they age, and we now have photographic proof that Evel Knievel came to his senses later in life.

While this topic may seem on the surface to be very lighthearted, there are deeper issues at play. If the wrong color boots are accepted, it just opens the floodgates to all sorts of emasculating behavior. One day, it's the wrong color boots; the next day, you'll see guys zipping their pants up on the side and carrying purses with eyeliner inside! All of manhood may stand at the crossroads of this critical issue! I cannot remain silent on this any longer. Someone must be the voice of reason! I cannot imagine William Wallace, Mr. T, or Rambo wearing white boots. So here is the final word from the top:

Real men wear black boots; *little girlie-men* wear white boots. 'Nuff said.[2]

THE MIRROR ON THE WALL

He who does not mind his belly will hardly mind anything else.[213]

—Samuel Johnson

I t does us no good if we become financially rich but poor in health. In our business, we talk about the 8 Fs—one of which is *fitness*. And while I have zero desire to be one of those guys you see in the Calvin Klein boxers ads who have three percent body fat (unless it took no effort and I didn't have to show people my boxers), I certainly do have a goal of living a long and healthy life.

When you do as much traveling around the country as my business partners and I do, it can become pretty easy to fall into some bad

---

2   Chris Brady says, "For those unfamiliar with this scandalous controversy, you may want to inquire about details with the author of the book *Rascal*."

eating habits. Now, these habits are enjoyable for the short-term, but they bring long-term pain and suffering. Most of my favorite negative health habits revolve around fast food.

I love food. Eating is like a sport to me. I love to treat myself to a Taco Bell, or some other fast-food, snack as a reward for a successful business meeting. In fact, I can wolf down a Burrito Supreme, burp a few times, and back to the races I go. In America, we don't portion our food. The "portion" is whatever is on the plate in front of me—times two. And I'm not like those skinny Europeans who walk everywhere they go and stay thin by nibbling on tofu all day.

In fact, I have to admit that at times, I have made fun of healthy people. I've even got a nickname for them: skinny-faced water drinkers. Any skinny, fit people who deny themselves the pleasure of a Wendy's Baconator with extra grease have got some serious issues! They don't know what they're missing!

One of the guys on my business team is a big bodybuilder and a fitness coach. He is a big dude; he could pick up a small car and toss it! I remember one time when my son Cameron was with us, and my bodybuilder friend climbed into the hot tub. Now, it became very apparent to me that I had two arms, and my friend had two arms. But they were very different. His pecs looked as though they were made of chiseled marble. My pecs looked as though they were made of marble cake. I told Cam not to look at my buddy – that that wasn't what *real men* looked like. I joked with my buddy, "Hey, you keep hanging around me, and I'll teach you how to have a body like mine!"

Well, after years of making fun of skinny, fit people and wolfing down as much truck-stop fast food as I could find, it shouldn't come as a big surprise that my bad habit started to catch up with me. One day, as I stared at myself in the mirror of my motorcoach, it really hit me. There was simply too much Tim Marks in the world. And most of the "too much" was centered on my big jiggly belly.

It's a little unnerving to have your tummy jiggle when you brush your teeth. At first I tried to justify it by telling myself, "Oh, it's probably that my mirror is distorted or something." But when my motorcoach was going down the road at sixty-five miles per hour, there was no way to avoid the truth: Every bump in the road jiggled that big pile of goo around my gut.

What was especially disappointing was that I had once been in really good shape back in my football days! I even had a six-pack back then. But now, my six-pack had transformed into a keg!

But the biggest shock of all was when I visited a chiropractor to have my neck adjusted. I was so totally out of shape I actually induced my chiropractor to take my blood pressure. He asked, "Tim, have you ever had high blood pressure before?" I said no. He told me I needed to get my blood pressure checked by my doctor because it didn't look good.

Up until then, I had always justified my weight. I would say, "I don't care if I'm overweight!" or "I can lose weight anytime I want!" or "My diet is balanced. I eat a microwaved healthy dinner every three days!" It's so easy to justify things to ourselves and make excuses. But when the doctor says you've got a problem, then, brother, it's time to listen.

I went to see my doctor, and of course, he is a skinny-faced water drinker. Normally, I would just crack jokes about this, but that day, he had my attention. I was willing to listen because I believe in learning from people who exhibit results. This guy was in shape and had spent years studying how the human body works. He was a doctor! It would have been pretty arrogant of me to dismiss his opinion.

My doctor gave me some bad news: My blood pressure was 184/127. "You're almost 250 pounds, Tim. You're obese," he said.

I said, "I'm not obese. You're delirious!" I shouldn't have disagreed with the doctor, but I did. Maybe I didn't want to believe what he was saying! Most of the time, we just ignore the advice of people who have the results we want. We make excuses for ourselves, to justify our behavior, but what we need to do is listen to a mentor. I have some friends whom I love very much who struggle with weight issues, but they choose to put their heads in the sand like an

> *Most of the time, we just ignore the advice of people who have the results we want.*

204

ostrich hiding from a lion. The problem is that doesn't change the lion's dinner plans! The lion is still going to get you!

My doctor said, "I'm going to put you on blood pressure medication. You need to start exercising. If we could get you down to 210 pounds, you'd be right at the point of overweight but healthy."

I protested at first, but then I realized he was right. I remembered that when I was 210 pounds, I felt much better than I had been feeling recently. I agreed I should start exercising. But as for the blood pressure medication, I wasn't sold yet.

"I don't need that medication," I told him. "I'll just start working out."

And this doctor said eight words that changed my life. He said, "No, you won't. You will stroke yourself out."

It was a pretty scary thought. But it was enough to scare me into action. I started taking his advice. I took the medication and started exercising. I decreased the calories in my daily diet. I started reading a book called *Body for Life* and followed its program.[214] I took the meds for less than a week and started a natural remedy. I lost seven pounds in the first week. In less than a month, through proper diet and exercise, I was down to a blood pressure reading of 122/68. A big improvement! And I was off the blood pressure pills.

Cyril Connolly said, "The one way to get thin is to reestablish a purpose in life."[215] I want to be a positive example to the people I work with, and you can't be a true success unless you are healthy. I know I am in a position of leadership, and leadership means more responsibility with less personal freedom. Because

> *I know I am in a position of leadership, and leadership means more responsibility with less personal freedom.*

my organization promotes fitness as a part of a successful life, it's literally my job as a leader to push aside some of those yummy treats. If we can discipline ourselves in the finance area, can't we apply the same discipline in the fitness area? I know my business organization will do only 50 percent of what I do right, and 100 percent of what I do wrong, as I've said before. That means the example I set has to be twice as good as what I expect from those under my leadership.

> *If we can discipline ourselves in the finance area, can't we apply the same discipline to the fitness area?*

I am by no means a fitness guru, nor do I ever plan on being one. But the smartest thing I did was recognize that I had a weight and health problem, and I followed the advice of the people who had the expertise and the results to back up their claims. We have only one body, and we need to treat it like a temple. All the money in the world won't matter if you're sick as a dog in the hospital! Ernest Hemingway said, "I still need more healthy rest in order to work at my best. My health is the main capital I have, and I want to administer it intelligently."[216] I hope you make a similar decision to start eating better, cut out the fast food and junk food, get some more exercise, and go to the doctor. Listen to the advice of people who have the results you want! Having that conversation with my doctor probably saved my life, and a similar conversation might save yours!

THE FAITH OF KEVIN JOHNSON

A red-hot belief in eternal glory is probably the best antidote to human panic that there is.[217]

—Phyllis Bottome

Kevin Johnson is an example of how our faith can sustain us during a major health challenge. When he faced horrible medical circumstances, Kevin Johnson completely believed in the possibility of a miracle in his life. To say he walked through the valley of darkness would be an understatement; he faced so many medical challenges and setbacks he shouldn't have lived through his ordeal the way he did. I believe the saving grace of God was what kept him alive when his body was failing him.[218]

Kevin made a life for himself in Mount Pleasant, Arkansas, and was basically living his life as a normal husband and father. He was a Christian and had previously been tested to be an organ donor. A little boy who had been fighting leukemia had needed a bone marrow transplant, and Kevin offered to be a donor for him. They discovered he wasn't a match, but not for lack of willingness on Kevin's part; he had a giving spirit to help other people. He was an advocate for people signing their driver's licenses to become donors, something that would prove to be critical when he faced his own hour of desperation.[219]

Kevin led an active life, playing golf and pickup basketball throughout his adult life. He was not as fit as he was when he played college basketball, but he was never sedentary. For a forty-two-year-old man, he was in shape and healthy, having never even been to a family doctor. In July of 2005, Kevin started to notice the onset of fatigue during a pickup basketball game at his work. He started to feel exhausted all the time.[220]

Doctors were stumped as to why this was happening, but after some tests, they noticed that something was wrong with Kevin's heart. With further testing, they had some numbers to share with Kevin—some very scary numbers. Normally, the heart squeezes out a certain amount of blood from each chamber when it pumps. The technical term for this is the ejection fraction, or EF. A normal heart has an EF of 55 percent to 70 percent. By the time they started to monitor Kevin, his EF had plummeted to 12 percent. His heart was barely keeping him alive.[221]

For the next nine months, Kevin lived in agony and misery. He dreaded the sun going down at night because he could barely sleep for fifteen minutes at a time. He had to sleep on his knees, with his chest on a footstool, all night long. He could barely breathe. The nights were long and dark, and pretty quickly, his faith was tested. He would pray with his wife Tammy for the Lord to take away his agony; he would say, "Lord, if you're not going to heal me, then please let me die."

Can you imagine being in so much physical pain that death might be something you looked forward to? That's where Kevin was. But he was always careful to throw the word *if* into his prayer, because if the Lord was going to heal him, he *did* want to live.[222]

Through his ordeal, Kevin's faith sustained him. And when I learned of his story, I was struck by how strong his faith truly was. He was blessed to have Tammy by his side, and her faith was equally strong.[223]

It soon became obvious that Kevin needed a new heart, but available hearts are in pretty big demand. In fact, the average waiting time to receive a heart for transplant is disheartening, no pun intended. It usually takes 248 days. And the sad truth is that a lot of people don't survive the wait. There are over one hundred thousand people in the United States waiting for an organ transplant to save their lives—whether from a problem with the heart, lungs, liver, kidneys, or pancreas—and only twenty-five thousand transplants are done a year. Six thousand people will die this year waiting for a transplant. That's almost one person every hour.[224]

Kevin's wife Tammy prayed with him and shared a verse—Mark 5:36: "Do not fear, only believe"(ESV). The Lord knew Kevin didn't have that long with an EF of 12 percent. Kevin went on the organ waiting list, but he didn't wait 248 days—only three. It was the second fastest match in the Arkansas medical history. In seventy-two hours, the phone rang. A fifty-one-year-old man named Wendell had passed, and because he had signed his organ donor card, Kevin's life would be spared.[225]

It takes only four hours for a heart to be harvested from the donor and then surgically implanted - four hours to get the heart out of the body of the deceased, onto a medical helicopter, and out to Kevin. Kevin prayed to God that there wouldn't be a wreck. The doctor tried to reassure him by half-joking that they wouldn't take Kevin's old heart out until the new one arrived. That was on Father's Day. One boy's dad passed away so that another boy's dad could live.[226]

When a person has an organ transplant from another body, it's normal for the body to fight back against the new organ and reject it, almost as if it is a disease. To stop this from happening, Kevin had to take a lot of pills each day — twenty pills a day, 600 pills a month, 7,200 pills a year. Kevin later joked that his pharmacist loved him – that he was the pharmacy's favorite customer![227]

At first, the new heart seemed fine. Kevin's EF zoomed up to 70 percent, and he started walking four miles a day. He felt great and figured he might finally be out of the woods. But this lasted for all of four months. In 120 days, his EF dropped to 45 percent. Eight weeks later, it was back down to 13 percent. His new heart was failing him, too.[228]

His doctors were stumped anew. They thought maybe his body was rejecting the heart, but that wasn't the case. Something else was going on. Then they started thinking Kevin could have a rare disease — the light chain deposition disease. That was bad news, but the bigger problem for Kevin was that if he had a disease, he wouldn't be eligible for another heart transplant. They just didn't give hearts to people who were going to die of a disease anyway; one needed to have a good chance of survival.[229]

After a stint at the Mayo clinic, Kevin was given the green light to receive a new heart. A seventeen-year-old boy named Justin who lived in Kentucky had passed away, and Kevin was the lucky recipient. Again, it looked as if Kevin was on the mend. And then that heart started to fail as well. Once again, his EF plummeted.[230]

Kevin prayed and prayed: "Lord Jesus, if you heal me, I won't waste this heart. I'm going to live for Jesus and make my life count. I won't waste another minute. My every breath is a gift from the Almighty God that I did not earn and do not deserve. It is a gift."[231]

The doctor said, "Your heart isn't getting better. It's scarred up, but I believe in miracles." And the doctor prayed with Kevin.[232]

A friend who was visiting said to Kevin, "Wow, you have an incredible attitude! What's the deal? Aren't you mad at God?"[233]

Kevin laughed and said, "If I'm getting ready to meet Him, why in the world would I be mad at Him? I want to get on good terms with Him! I want Him to say, 'Hello, Kevin. I just talked to you this morning!' I don't want Him to say, 'Hey, you haven't prayed or read your Bible in weeks, and you haven't been talking to Me!'" Kevin's faith was unshakable. He realized that it was better to die with some hope than have no hope at all. Hope is a great thing, indeed.[234]

During this time, a friend sent Kevin a Charles Sturgeon devotional, and he had marked it at 2 Chronicles 16:9. "For the eyes of the Lord run to and fro throughout the whole Earth, to give strong support to those whose heart is blameless toward Him" (ESV). Kevin said to his wife, "That's a great verse! Let's claim that verse as ours today."[235]

That afternoon, one of Kevin's best friends called him and said, "I've got a great verse for you! And it was 2 Chronicles 16:9. Kevin laughed and told him it was just like God to do this, that he had just read that verse that same morning. Out of thirty-three thousand verses, what kind of a coincidence was it that he and his friend focused on the same verse that day?[236]

Late that night, a little nurse from Ireland walked into Kevin's hospital room to check on him. She said, "Kevin, the eyes of the Lord run to and fro throughout the whole Earth, to give strong support to those whose heart is blameless toward Him." And Kevin wept, knowing his life was truly in God's hands.[237]

Soon thereafter, the doctor called in all of her nurses. Normally, this would be a very bad thing, but she said, "Kevin, your EF is 56 percent. It's a miracle. Nobody thought you would ever walk out of here." Then she turned to her nurses: "If you ever know someone who needs confirmation of a miracle, you are looking at one right here."[238]

Throughout Kevin's ordeal, he faced more medical challenges in one lifetime than twenty men normally would. What he experienced reads like a laundry list of everything a person could go through:

- 4 ambulance rides
- 1 helicopter med flight
- 2 jet med flights to the Mayo Clinic
- 6 med flights to the Texas Heart Institute
- admission to 8 different hospitals
- 232 days in hospitals
- hundreds of blood draws

- countless IVs
- 50–100 X-rays
- 11 MRIs: 8 heart, 2 bone, 1 brain
- PET scans, CAT scans
- high blood pressure, low blood pressure, and zero blood pressure
- weight loss of 22 lbs. in 12 hours, a record at Baptist Intensive Care
- weight loss of 43 lbs. of fluid in 48 hours
- coughing up blood
- lung fluid drained twice
- a collapsed lung
- a chest tube
- 2 scopes in the lungs
- inability to breathe and sleep
- placed on oxygen
- BiPAP machine
- sleep apnea
- fatigue beyond description (He literally could not walk 100 feet at the height of his disease.)
- possibility of either of the following: lung cancer, myeloma, lymphoma, amyloidosis of the heart, and light chain deposition disease
- heart failure, 3 times
- atrial fibrillation
- V-tach rhythm
- shocked back into rhythm with the paddles 6 times
- defibrillator in the heart
- external defibrillator in a vest for 3 months, slept with it 24 hours a day
- severe withdrawal from pain medications
- skin cancer caused by rejection medication for the transplanted hearts
- 5 arteriograms
- 12 chemo treatments

- 10 massive steroid treatments
- 12 plasma treatments
- 6 bone marrow draws
- almost a year in isolation due to a low immune system, wearing a mask and gloves
- 2 kidney biopsies
- 30 heart biopsies
- 3 strokes (in which he lost use of his left eye and the right side of his body, but the use of these was later, miraculously, restored)
- 2 heart transplants[239]

Through it all, he credited his faith in the Lord with sustaining him. After his ordeal, he lived long enough to go back to work, to sleep like a baby, and begin playing golf again. He attended his daughter's college graduation, celebrated his twenty-seventh wedding anniversary, and was there for his son when he went through brain surgery. Ever since he got sick, Kevin got to watch the sun set over the Pacific and in the Caribbean. He never missed a sunset. When it rained, he loved the feeling of the raindrops on his face. He got to teach his young son to ride a bike. Every night, he got to kiss his beautiful wife good night. And every day, he got to share the story of God's grace in his life.[240]

Zig Ziglar says, "I *like* the things that money *can* buy, but I *love* the things that money *can't* buy. Money can buy a house, but not a home. Money can buy a doctor, but it can't buy health. Money can buy a clock, but it can't buy time. Money can buy a bed, but it cannot buy a good night's sleep."[241]

> *Money can buy a house, but not a home. Money can buy a doctor, but it can't buy health. Money can buy a clock, but it can't buy time. Money can buy a bed, but it cannot buy a good night's sleep.*
> *— Zig Ziglar*

Kevin said, "Three people have died so that I could live: a fifty-one-year-old man named Wendell, a seventeen-year-old boy named Justin, and a thirty-three-year-old carpenter named Jesus. The first two didn't die for me on purpose, but the last one did, and I'm thankful for all three of them."[242]

And this year, Kevin passed away to finally be with his Lord. Through everything, he was passionate in his faith, and this is the point I want to make: He was relentlessly passionate in his faith. A lot of people think it's horrible that the disease finally won and he died, but his wife Tammy would testify to his sustaining love for and happiness in the Lord.[243]

Everybody dies. I'm going to die, and you are going to die. Little babies die, teenagers die, moms and dads die, and although some people make it past one hundred, they still die. God says we have an appointment to meet Him, and we're going to keep that appointment. My point is not how you die, but how you live. Live with faith and hope and love. Live your life like the Tim McGraw song "Live Like You Were Dying."[244] Kevin Johnson lived a more passionate life than many people because he saw every minute as a gift, and I have been inspired by the story of his faith in and passion for the Lord. I hope it touches you in the same way.

CONCLUSION

Happy is he who still loves something he loved in the nursery: He has not been broken in two by time; he is not two men, but one, and he has saved not only his soul, but his life.[245]

—Gilbert K. Chesterton

L ife is meant to be lived fully. I believe that true success comes from abundance in every area of life, including your faith, friendships, fun, and fitness. As we each pursue our personal and professional goals, I hope that you are reminded to nurture your friendships, cherish your health, and love your Lord. Robert Brault

213

said, "Enjoy the little things, for one day you may look back and realize they were the big things."[246] Being in good health and able to run and throw the football with my son Cam may seem like a little thing to some, but it's actually a big thing. Having friends whom I can share the great adventures of life with may seem like a small thing, but it's a big thing. Spending time in prayer each morning may seem like a small thing, but it's a big thing—it's the biggest thing.

KEY POINTS

1. As Stephen Covey says, sharpen your saw. If you want to be your personal best in all 8 Fs of life, you need to take time for renewal.

2. Nurture your friendships. Friendships make every victory sweeter to enjoy and every setback easier to endure.

3. Have *fun*. Don't take yourself too seriously. Make time to smell the roses and hunt down the tarpon-eating sharks.

4. Your body is a temple. You can deceive yourself, but not the mirror. Most people dig their graves with a fork.

5. Leaders should set the example for others in the area of fitness. If I can discipline myself when it comes to my finances, surely I can discipline myself with my fitness. The people I lead may only do half of what I do, so I must do twice as much as I hope to see them do for themselves.

6. Faith will carry you through every trial including health challenges. Have the faith of Kevin Johnson.

EPILOGUE

Knowing is not enough; we must apply. Willing is not enough; we must do.[247]

—Johann Wolfgang von Goethe

I hope you've enjoyed this book and that my experiences may be of some value to you. As my business partners like to say, "The best way to go through a minefield is to follow someone else." The best experience is truly someone else's because it saves you time, and you can avoid making the same mistakes that person made. As you have read, I have made many mistakes in my life, and more than anything, I hope you choose to avoid making mine!

But a book like this is simply entertaining unless you choose to do something about its message. And that really is my parting message to you: Choose what you want your life to be. You do have that ability to define what you want, learn how to do it, and then take action. Sadly, few people follow through on this, but I hope you are one of the rare and amazing people who learn something positive and try to immediately apply it.

So what have you learned, and what are you going to apply? I challenge you to go back through the book and think about the ideas and lessons I have shared and really ask yourself whether you are living up to your personal best. For a long time in my life, I wasn't. I had to look at myself in the mirror and admit that the Tim Marks that I was just simply wasn't the Tim Marks I wanted to be. I saw good men around me, godly men who inspired me to raise my standards. And I've tried every day since then to follow their example.

As we conclude our time together, I want to share some final words of wisdom from a man I hold in high esteem, Coach John Wooden. He is the college-basketball coach with the greatest winning record. He is also an incredible human being. In his book *Wooden: A Lifetime of Observations and Reflections On and Off the Court,* he shared how on the day of his graduation, his dad gave him a card with his father's creed, which he called "Seven Things to Do." Here they are:

1. Be true to yourself.
2. Help others.
3. Make each day your masterpiece.
4. Drink deeply from good books, especially the Bible.
5. Make friendship a fine art.
6. Build a shelter against a rainy day.
7. Pray for guidance and count and give thanks for your blessings every day.[248]

I love this creed, and it's such an important part of our family culture that my kids have it memorized. You may choose to memorize it as well. I can tell you that it certainly has guided me.

What do you want for yourself and your ideal life? What do you want for each of these areas: faith, family, finance, fitness, freedom, following, friendship, and fun? I recommend that you set goals for each and go after them using the ideas we've discussed in this book. And I suggest following the advice of Pastor Tom Ascol: "Be a real Christian, and act like it."

I was asked by an interviewer once what I would tell my kids if I were dying in the hospital and had to share a few final words of wisdom and encouragement. I thought about it for a moment, and the answer came pretty easily—because it's what I believe: Define what you want, learn from someone who has gone before you, and then do it for the glory of God.

NOTES

Forward

1   Orrin Woodward, *RESOLVED: 13 Resolutions for LIFE* (Flint: Obstacles Press, 2011).

Introduction

2   Miguell De Cervantes, "Quotation Center," 2009, accessed July 26, 2011, http://www.cybernation.com.

3   Jeff Shaara, Michael Shaara, and Ronald F. Maxwell, *Gods and Generals*, Ronald F. Maxwell, Producer/Director/Screenwriter (Warner Bros., Released February 21, 2003).

4   Ibid.

Chapter One

5   Brian Klemmer, *Compassionate Samurai: Being Extraordinary in an Ordinary World* (New York: Hay House, 2008).

6   George Lucas, *Star Wars*, Directed by George Lucas (Twentieth Century Fox, Released May 25, 1977).

7   Og Mandino, *The Greatest Salesman in the World* (New York: Bantam Books, 1985).

8   William Carey, "ThinkExist Quotation Database," acessed October 9, 2011, http://www.thinkexist.com.

9   Sidney A. Friedman, "Quotation Center," 2009, accessed

September 26, 2011, http://www.cybernation.com.

10   Sigmund Freud, "Quotation Center," 2009, accessed September 26, 2011, http://www.cybernation.com.

11   Horace, "Quotation Center," 2009, accessed September 26, 2011, http://www.cybernation.com.

12   Jean Paul Richter, "Quotation Center," 2009, accessed September 26, 2011, http://www.cybernation.com.

13   Eleanor Roosevelt, "Quotation Center," 2009, accessed September 26, 2011, http://www.cybernation.com.

14   Christopher D. Furman, "Quotation Center," 2009, accessed September 26, 2011, http://www.cybernation.com.

15   Vince Lombardi, "Quotation Center," 2009, accessed September 26, 2011, http://www.cybernation.com.

16   Anatole France, "Quotation Center," 2009, accessed September 26, 2011, http://www.cybernation.com.

17   Paul Boese, "Quotation Center," 2009, accessed September 26, 2011, http://www.cybernation.com.

18   Michael Wilson and Rod Serling, *Planet of the Apes*, Directed by Franklin J. Shaffner (Twentieth Century Fox, Released April 3, 1968).

19   Tracy L. McNair, "Quotation Center," 2009, accessed November 17, 2011, http://www.cybernation.com.

Chapter Two

20   Tryon Edwards, "Quotation Center," 2009, accessed September 26, 2011, www.cybernation.com.

21   Jerry Siegel, Joe Shuster, and Mario Puzo, *Superman: The Movie*, Directed by Richard Donner (Warner Bros., Released December 17, 1978).

22   Sir Walter Scott, "Quotation Center," 2009, accessed September 26, 2011, http://www.cybernation.com.

23   Robert E. Lee, "Quotation Center," 2009, accessed September 26, 2011, http://www.cybernation.com.

24   Pablo Picasso, "Quotation Center," 2009, accessed September 26, 2011, http://www.cybernation.com.

25   John Jensen, "Quotation Center," 2009, accessed September 26, 2011, http://www.cybernation.com.

26   Zig Ziglar, "BrainyQuote," 2012, accessed September 26, 2011, http://www.brainyquote.com.

27   John C. Maxwell, *The 21 Irrefutable Laws of Leadership: Follow Them and People Will Follow You*. 10th Anniversary Ed. (Nashville: Thomas Nelson Publishers, 2007), 134.

28   Zig Ziglar, "Goals," Cassette Tape, Produced by Nightingale-Conant Audio.

29   Ibid.

30   Ibid.

31   Ibid.

32   Ibid.

33   Ibid.

34   Ibid.

35   Ibid.

36   Ibid.

37   Ibid.

38   Ibid.

39   Ibid.

40   Ibid.

41   Jerry W. McCant, "Quotation Center," 2009, accessed September 26, 2011, http://www.cybernation.com.

42   Ralph Waldo Emerson, "Quotation Center," 2009, accessed September 26, 2011, http://www.cybernation.com.

43   Robert T. Kiyosaki and Sharon L. Lechter, *Cashlow Quadrant* (New York: Warner Books, 1999).

44   George Allen, "Quotation Center," 2009, accessed September 26, 2011, http://www.cybernation.com.

Chapter Three

45   David J. Schwartz, *The Magic of Thinking Big* (New York: Simon & Schuster, 1987).

46   Jim Collins, *Good to Great: Why Some Companies Make the Leap and Others Don't* (New York: HarperCollins Publishers, 2001).

47   Orison Swett Marden, "Quotation Center," 2009, accessed August 29, 2011, http://www.cybernation.com.

48   Else Roesdahl, *The Vikings: Revised Edition* (London: Penguin Books, 1998), 9.

49   Roesdahl, *The Vikings: Revised Edition*, 192.

50   Roesdahl, *The Vikings: Revised Edition*, 4.

51   Gwyn Jones, *A History of the Vikings* (Oxford: New York, 2001), 150.

52   Roesdahl, *The Vikings: Revised Edition*, 56.

53   Jones, *A History of the Vikings* (Oxford: New York, 2001), 148.

54   Jones, *A History of the Vikings*, 1.

55   Jones, *A History of the Vikings*, 196.

56   Roesdahl, *The Vikings: Revised Edition*, 3–4.

57   Andre Gide, "Quotation Center, "2009, accessed August 29, 2011, http://www.cybernation.com.

58   *Wikipedia*, s.v. "Harald Bluetooth," http://en.wikipedia.org/wiki/Harald_I_of_Denmark (accessed August 29, 2011).

59   Jones, *A History of the Vikings*, 126.

60   Roesdahl, *The Vikings: Revised Edition*, 80.

61   Iba Ezra, "Quotation Center," 2009, accessed August 29, 2011, http://www.cybernation.com.

62   Lawrence G. Lovasik, "BrainyQuote," 2012, accessed August 29, 2011, http://www.brainyquote.com.

63   Daniel Boorstin, "BrainyQuote," 2012, accessed August 29, 2011, http://www.brainyquote.com.

64   Saint Teresa of Avila, "BrainyQuote," 2012, accessed August 29, 2011, http://www.brainyquote.com.

65   Roesdahl, *The Vikings: Revised Edition*, 62.

66   Ibid.

67   Matthew Arnold, "Quotation Center," 2009, accessed August 29, 2011, http://www.cybernation.com.

68   Giovanna Garcia, "Giovanna Garcia's Website on Taking Imperfect Action," accessed August 29, 2011, http://www.imperfectaction.com.

69   Henry S. Haskins, "The Quote Garden: A Harvest of Quotes for Word Lovers," Phoenix: Terri Guillemets, 2011, accessed August 29, 2011, http://www.quotegarden.com.

70   Bethany Hamilton, "Soul Surfer: My Story" (Silicon Valley: Global Media Outreach, 2011), accessed August 29, 2011, http://soulsurfer.com/story/html.

71   Ibid.

72   Ibid.

73   Ibid.

74   Ibid.

75   Frederick W. Cropp, "Quotation Center," 2009, accessed August 29, 2011, http://www.cybernation.com.

76   Paul J. Meyer, "Quotation Center," 2009, accessed August 29, 2011, http://www.cybernation.com.

77   *Wikipedia*,   "Focus," accessed September 12, 2011, http://en.wikipedia.org/wiki/Focus.

78   Stephen B. Stokl, M.D., *Mentally Speaking* (Kitchener, Ontario: Volumes Publishing, 2006).

79   Ben Johnson, "Quotation Center," 2009, accessed August 29, 2011, http://www.cybernation.com.

80   John C. Maxwell, *The 21 Irrefutable Laws of Leadership: Follow Them*

and People Will Follow You, 10th Anniversary Ed. (Nashville: Thomas Nelson, 2007), 134.

81   Ralph Waldo Emerson, "Quotation Center," 2009, accessed August 29, 2011, http://www.cybernation.com.

82   Sir Isaac Newton, "Quotation Center," 2009, accessed August 29, 2011, http://www.cybernation.com.

83   Alex Kendrick and Stephen Kendrick, *Facing the Giants*, DVD, Directed by Alex Kendrick (Albany, GA: Sherwood Pictures, 2006).

84   Ibid.

85   Ibid.

86   Ibid.

87   Ibid.

88   Ibid.

89   Ibid.

90   Ibid.

Chapter Four

91   Winston Churchill, "Quotation Center," 2009, accessed August 16, 2011, http://www.cybernation.com.

92   Tom Kiatipis, "The Great Canadian Boot Camp," Speech (London, Ontario, Canada, August 4, 2011).

93   George Lucas, *Star Wars: The Empire Strikes Back*, DVD, Directed by Irvin Kershner (Twentieth Century Fox, 2004 – Originally released in theaters May 21, 1980).

94   Robert Fritz, "Quotation Center," 2009, accessed August 16, 2011,

http://www.cybernation.com.

95   Harry Emerson Fosdick, "Quotation Center," 2009, accessed August 16, 2011, http://www.cybernation.com.

96   Peter Marshall, "Quotation Center," 2009, accessed August 16, 2011, http://www.cybernation.com.

97   John W. Foster, "Quotation Center," 2009, accessed August 16, 2011, http://www.cybernation.com.

98   Vince Poscente, "ThinkExist Quotation Database," accessed August 16, 2011, http://www.thinkexist.com.

99   Joe Frazier, "Search Quotes Website," accessed August 16, 2011, http://www.searchquotes.com.

100   Don Yaeger, "The Most Important Golf Story of the Year (That You Likely Never Heard About)," *Success Magazine*, September 2010.

101   Ibid.

102   Ibid.

103   Ibid.

104   Ibid.

105   Curtis Grant, "Quotation Center," 2009, accessed August 16, 2011, http://www.cybernation.com.

106   Ram Charan and Larry Bossidy, *Execution: The Discipline of Getting Things Done* (New York: Crown Business, 2002).

107   Dale Carnegie, *How to Win Friends and Influence People* (New York: Simon & Schuster, 2009).

108   Les Giblin, *How to Have Confidence and Power in Dealing with People* (New York: Reward Books, 1956).

109 John Master, "Tom Peters Company Website," accessed August 10, 2011, http://www.tompeters.com.

110 Ralph Waldo Emerson, "Quotation Center," 2009, accessed August 16, 2011, http://www.cybernation.com.

111 Charles A. Garfield, "Quotation Center," 2009, accessed August 10, 2011, http://www.cybernation.com.

112 Jim Collins, *Good to Great: Why Some Companies Make the Leap and Others Don't* (New York: HarperCollins Publishers, 2001).

113 Kerry Patterson et al., *Influencer: The Power to Change Anything* (New York: VitalSmarts, 2008).

114 Brian Tracy, *Eat That Frog!* (San Francisco: Berrett-Khoehler Publishers, 2007).

115 *Wikipedia*, "Steve Jobs," accessed August 18, 2011, http://en.wikipedia.org/wiki/Steve_Jobs.

116 Ibid.

117 Lou Holtz, "Quotation Collection," accessed August 10, 2011, http://www.quotationcollection.com/author/Lou_Holtz/quotes.

118 Thomas J. Watson, "Quotation Center," 2009, accessed August 16, 2011, http://www.cybernation.com.

119 Sam Walton, *Sam Walton: Made in America* (New York: Bantam Books, 1993).

120 Tony Robbins, "Speech at the *Unleash the Power Within* Seminar" (Toronto, Canada, July 25, 2007).

121 Ibid.

122 Ibid.

123　John C. Maxwell, *The Success Journey: The Process of Living Your Dreams* (Nashville: Thomas Nelson Publishers, 1997).

124　Gael Boardman, "Quotation Center," 2009, accessed August 16, 2011 http://www.cybernation.com.

125　Scott Belsky, *Making Ideas Happen: Overcoming the Obstacles Between Vision and Reality* (New York: Penguin Group, 2010).

126　Malcolm Gladwell, *Outliers: The Story of Success* (New York: Little, Brown and Company, 2008).

127　Jim Collins, *Good to Great*.

128　Seth Godin, *Linchpin: Are You Indispensable?* (New York: Penguin Group, 2010).

129　H. Jackson Brown Jr., "Quotation Center," 2009, accessed August 16, 2011, http://www.cybernation.com.

130　Orrin Woodward, *RESOLVED*.

131　"Mary Lou Retton – Olympic Visions," accessed September 15, 2011, http://sports.jrank.org/pages/3829/Retton-Mary-Lou-Olympic-Visions.html.

132　Don Wilder and Bill Rechin, "The Quote Garden: A Harvest of Quotes for Word Lovers" (Phoenix: Terri Guillemets, 2011), accessed August 29, 2011, http://www.quotegarden.com.

133　Edward R. Murrow, "ThinkExist Quotation Database," accessed August 3, 2011, http://www.thinkexist.com.

134　"Benoit Lecomte: Quite a Guy," accessed August 3, 2011, http://www.legendinc.com/Pages/ArchivesCentral/COTDArchives/1998/10198.html.

135　Ibid.

136 Ibid.

137 Ibid.

138 Robert Brault, "The Quote Garden: A Harvest of Quotes for Word Lovers" (Phoenix: Terri Guillemets, 2011), accessed August 29, 2011, http://www.quotegarden.com.

139 "Patrick Henry Hughes – Inspirational Story," accessed August 3, 2011, http://www.youtube.com/watch?v=-qTiYA1WiY8.

140 Ibid.

141 Ibid.

142 Ibid.

143 Ibid.

144 Christian Nestell Bovee, "Quotation Center," 2009, accessed August 16, 2011, http://www.cybernation.com.

145 Bill Hybels, *Axiom: Powerful Leadership Proverbs* (Grand Rapids, MI: Zondervan, 2008).

146 Woodrow Wilson, "Quotation Center," 2009, accessed August 16, 2011, http://www.cybernation.com.

147 Brian Tracy, *Eat That Frog!* (San Francisco: Berrett-Khoehler Publishers, 2007).

148 Napoleon Hill, "Quotation Center," 2009, accessed August 16, 2011, http://www.cybernation.com.

149 Brian Tracy, *Eat That Frog!*

150 Charles Richards, "Quotation Center," 2009, accessed August 16, 2011, http://www.cybernation.com.

151 Stephen R. Covey, *First Things First* (New York: Free Press, 2003).

152 Antonio Porchia, "The Quote Garden: A Harvest of Quotes for Word Lovers" (Phoenix: Terri Guillemets, 2011), accessed August 16, 2011, http://www.quotegarden.com.

153 George Bernard Shaw, "Quotation Center," 2009, accessed August 16, 2011, http://www.cybernation.com.

154 Tony Robbins, "Speech at the *Unleash the Power Within* Seminar" (Toronto, Canada, July 25, 2007).

155 Edward R. Murrow, "ThinkExist Quotation Database, "accessed August 3, 2011, http://www.thinkexist.com.

Chapter Five

156 Mary Anne Radmacher, "ThinkExist Quotation Database," accessed September 1, 2011, http://www.thinkexist.com.

157 Annie Besant, "Quotation Center," 2009, accessed August 20, 2011, http://www.cybernation.com.

158 Steve Jobs, "Commencement Address to Stanford University on June 12, 2005," Accessed on August 20, 2011, http://news.stanford.edu/news/2005/june15/jobs-061505.html.

159 *Wikipedia*, "Steve Jobs," accessed August 18, 2011, http://en.wikipedia.org/wiki/Steve_Jobs.

160 Ibid.

161 Ibid.

162 Ibid.

163 Ibid.

164 Ibid.

165 George Lucas, *Star Wars*, Directed by George Lucas (Twentieth Century Fox, Released May 25, 1977).

166 Ibid.

167 Ibid.

168 Ibid.

169 Ibid.

170 Ibid.

171 Ibid.

172 John Maxwell, *Your Road Map for Success: You Can Get There from Here* (Nashville: Thomas Nelson Publishers, 2006).

173 L. Thomas Holdcroft, "Quotation Center," 2009, accessed August 20, 2011, http://www.cybernation.com.

174 Hellen Keller, "Quotation Center," 2009, accessed August 20, 2011, http://www.cybernation.com.

175 Tommy Newbury, *Success Is Not an Accident* (Decatur, GA: Looking Glass Books, 1999).

176 C.J. Mahaney, *Humility: True Greatmess* (Colorado Springs: Multnomah Publishers, 2005).

177 James C. Collins, *How the Mighty Fall: And Why Some Companies Never Give In* (New York: HarperCollins Publishers, 2009).

178 Charles Spurgeon, "Spurgeon's Maxims for Living," http://www.spurgeon.us/quotes.htm.

179 Samuel Johnson, "ThinkExist Quotation Database," accessed August 20, 2011, http://www.thinkexist.com.

180 Eileen Caddy, "Quotation Center," 2009, accessed August 20, 2011, http://www.cybernation.com.

181 James Whitcomb, "Quotation Center," 2009, accessed August 20, 2011, http://www.cybernation.com.

182 Norman Vincent Peale, "Quotation Center," 2009, accessed August 20, 2011, http://www.cybernation.com.

183 *Wikipedia*, "John Grisham," accessed on August 19, 2011, http://en.wikipedia.org/wiki/John_Grisham.

184 Ibid.

185 Ibid.

186 Ibid.

187 Ibid.

188 Ibid.

189 Ibid.

190 Ibid.

191 Ibid.

192 Ibid.

193 Ibid.

194 Henry David Thoreau, "ThinkExist Quotation Database," accessed August 20, 2011, http://www.thinkexist.com.

195 *Wikipedia*, "Károly Takács," accessed on August 19, 2011, http://www.en.wikipedia.org/wiki/K%C3%A1roly _Tak%C3%A1cs.

196 Ibid.

197 Ibid.

198 Ibid.

199 Ibid.

200 Ibid.

201 Ibid.

202 Ibid.

203 Ibid.

204 General George S. Patton, "Quotation Center," 2009, accessed August 20, 2011, http://www.cybernation.com.

205 Norman Vincent Peale, "Quotation Center," 2009, accessed August 20, 2011, http://www.cybernation.com.

206 John Lasseter and Joe Ranft, *Cars*, Directed by John Lasseter and Joe Ranft (Walt Disney Studios and Pixar Animation Studios, Released June 9, 2006).

Chapter Six

207 Joseph Addison, "Quotation Center," 2009, accessed September 24, 2011, http://www.cybernation.com.

208 Stephen R. Covey, *The 7 Habits of Highly Effective People* (New York: Fireside, 1990).

209 St. Thomas Aquinas, "Quotation Center," 2009, accessed September 24, 2011, http://www.cybernation.com.

210 Rich DiGirolamo, "Quotation Center," 2009, accessed September 24, 2011, http://www.cybernation.com.

211   Joseph Addison, "Quotation Center," 2009, accessed September 24, 2011, http://www.cybernation.com.

212   Peter Benchley, *Jaws*, Directed by Steven Spielberg (Universal Studios, Released June 20, 1975).

213   Samuel Johnson, "Quotation Center," 2009, accessed September 24, 2011, http://www.cybernation.com.

214   Bill Phillips, *Body for Life: 12 Weeks to Mental and Physical Strength* (New York: HarperCollins, 1999).

215   Cyril Connolly, "Quotation Center," 2009, accessed September 24, 2011, http://www.cybernation.com.

216   Ernest Hemingway, "Quotation Center," 2009, accessed September 24, 2011, http://www.cybernation.com.

217   Phyllis Bottome, "Quotation Center," 2009, accessed September 24, 2011, http://www.cybernation.com.

218   Kevin Johnson, "Jesus Is Still the One," DVD, Recorded at Marrable Hill Chapel Church in El Dorado, Arkansas on Father's Day, June 21, 2009.

219   Ibid.

220   Ibid.

221   Ibid.

222   Ibid.

223   Ibid.

224   Ibid.

225   Ibid.

226 Ibid.

227 Ibid.

228 Ibid.

229 Ibid.

230 Ibid.

231 Ibid.

232 Ibid.

233 Ibid.

234 Ibid.

235 Ibid.

236 Ibid.

237 Ibid.

238 Ibid.

239 Ibid.

240 Ibid.

241 Zig Ziglar, *Over the Top* (Nashville: Thomas Nelson, 1997).

242 Kevin Johnson, "Jesus Is Still the One."

243 Ibid.

244 Tim McGraw, "Live Like You Were Dying," Written by Tim Nichols and Wiseman, Title track on *Live Like You Were Dying* album (Curb Records, Released August 24, 2004).

245 Gilbert K. Chesterton, "Quotation Center," 2009, accessed November 17, 2011, http://www.cybernation.com.

246 Robert Brault, "Quotation Center," 2009, accessed September 24, 2011, http://www.cybernation.com.

Epilogue

247 Johann Wolfgang von Goethe, "Quotation Center," 2009, accessed September 24, 2011, http://www.cybernation.com.

248 John Wooden, *Wooden: A Lifetime of Observations and Reflections On and Off the Court* (New York: McGraw-Hill, 1997).

BIBLIOGRAPHY

Belsky, Scott. *Making Ideas Happen: Overcoming the Obstacles Between Vision and Reality*. New York: Penguin Group, 2010.

Benchley, Peter. *Jaws*. Directed by Steven Spielberg. Universal Studios, Released June 20, 1975.

BookRags Media Network. "Zig Ziglar Quotation." BrainyQuote. 2012. http://www.brainyquote.com.

Bossidy, Larry and Ram Charan. *Execution: The Discipline of Getting Things Done*. NewYork: Crown Business, 2002.

Brady, Chris. *Rascal: Making a Difference by Becoming an Original Character*. Flint: Obstacles Press, 2010.

Carnegie, Dale. *How to Win Friends and Influence People*. New York: Simon & Schuster, 2009.

Collins, James C. *Good to Great: Why Some Companies Make the Leap and Others Don't*. New York: HarperCollins Publishers, 2001.

Collins, James C. *How the Mighty Fall: And Why Some Companies Never Give In*. New York: HarperCollins Publishers, 2009.

Covey, Stephen R. *First Things First*. New York: Free Press, 2003.

Covey, Stephen R. *The 7 Habits of Highly Effective People*. New York: Fireside, 1990.

Cyber Nation International. "Famous Quotations." Quotation Center. 2009. http://www.cybernation.com.

Garcia, Giovanna. "Giovanna Garcia's Website on Taking Imperfect Action." Accessed August 29, 2011. http://www.imperfectaction. com.

Giblin, Les. *How to Have Confidence and Power in Dealing with People.* New York: Reward Books, 1956.

Gladwell, Malcolm. *Outliers: The Story of Success.* New York: Little, Brown and Company, 2008.

Godin, Seth. *Linchpin: Are You Indispensable?*(New York: Penguin Group, 2010).

Guillemets, Terri. "The Quote Garden: A Harvest of Quotes for Word Lovers." Phoenix: Terri Guillemets, 2011. Accessed August 29, 2011. http://www.quotegarden.com.

Hamilton, Bethany. "Soul Surfer: My Story." Silicon Valley: Global Media Outreach, 2011. Accessed August 29, 2011. http://soulsurfer. com/story/html.

Hill, Napoleon. *Think and Grow Rich.* Tribeca Books, 2011.

Holtz, Lou. "Quotation Collection." Accessed August 10, 2011. http:// www.quotationcollection.com/author/Lou_Holtz/quotes.

Hybels, Bill. *Axiom: Powerful Leadership Proverbs.* Grand Rapids, MI: Zondervan, 2008.

Jobs, Steve. "Commencement Address to Stanford University on June 12, 2005." Accessed on August 20, 2011. http://news.stanford. edu/news/2005/june15/jobs-061505.html.

Kevin Johnson, "Jesus Is Still the One," DVD, Recorded at Marrable Hill Chapel Church in El Dorado, Arkansas on Father's Day, June 21, 2009.

Kiatipis, Tom. "The Great Canadian Boot Camp." Speech. London, Ontario, Canada, August 4, 2011.

Jones, Gwyn. *A History of the Vikings*. Oxford: New York, 2001.

Kendrick, Alex and Stephen Kendrick. *Facing the Giants*. DVD. Directed by Alex Kendrick. Albany, GA: Sherwood Pictures, 2006.

Kiyosaki, Robert T. and Sharon L. Lechter. *Cashflow Quadrant*. New York: Warner Books, 1999.

Klemmer, Brian. *Compassionate Samurai: Being Extraordinary in an Ordinary World*. New York: Hay House, 2008.

Lasseter, John and Joe Ranft. *Cars*. Directed by John Lasseter and Joe Ranft. Walt Disney Studios and Pixar Animation Studios, Released June 9, 2006.

Legend Advertising. "Benoit Lecomte: Quite a Guy." Accessed August 3, 2011. http://www.legendinc.com/Pages/ArchivesCentral/COTDArchives/1998/10198.html.

Lucas, George. *Star Wars: The Empire Strikes Back*. DVD. Directed by Irvin Kershner. Twentieth Century Fox, 2004 – Originally released in theaters May 21, 1980.

Lucas, George. *Star Wars*. Directed by George Lucas. Twentieth Century Fox, Released May 25, 1977.

Mahaney, C.J. *Humility: True Greatness*. Colorado Springs: Multnomah Publishers, 2005.

Mandino, Og. *The Greatest Salesman in the World.* New York: Bantam Books, 1985.

Maxwell, John C. *The 21 Irrefutable Laws of Leadership: Follow Them and People Will Follow You.* 10th Anniversary Ed. Nashville: Thomas Nelson Publishers, 2007.

Maxwell, John C. *The Success Journey: The Process of Living Your Dreams.* Nashville: Thomas Nelson Publishers, 1997.

Maxwell, John C. *Your Road Map to Success: You Can Get There from Here.* Nashville: Thomas Nelson Publishers, 2006.

McGraw, Tim. "Live Like You Were Dying." Written by Tim Nichols and Wiseman. Title track on *Live Like You Were Dying* album. Curb Records, Released August 24, 2004.

Net Industries. "Mary Lou Retton – Olympic Visions." Accessed September 15, 2011. http://sports.jrank.org/pages/3829/Retton-Mary-Lou-Olympic-Visions.html.

Newbury, Tommy. *Success Is Not an Accident.* Decatur, GA: Looking Glass Books, 1999.

Patterson, Kerry, Joseph Grenny, David Maxfield, Ron McMillan, and Al Switzler. *Influencer: The Power to Change Anything.* New York: VitalSmarts, 2008.

Phillips, Bill. *Body for Life: 12 Weeks to Mental and Physical Strength.* New York: HarperCollins, 1999.

Robbins, Tony. "Speech at the *Unleash the Power Within* Seminar." Toronto, Canada, July 25, 2007.

Roesdahl, Else. *The Vikings: Revised Edition.* London: Penguin Books, 1998.

Schwartz, David J. *The Magic of Thinking Big*. New York: Simon & Schuster, 1987.

"Search Quotes Website." Accessed August 16, 2011. http://www.searchquotes.com

Shaara, Michael, Jeff Shaara, and Ronald Maxwell. *Gods and Generals*. Ron Maxwell, Producer/Director/Screenwriter. Warner Bros., Released February 21, 2003.

Siegel, Jerry, Joe Shuster, and Mario Puzo. *Superman: The Movie*. Directed by Richard Donner. Warner Bros., Released December 17, 1978.

Stokl, Stephen B., M.D. *Mentally Speaking*. Kitchener, Ontario: Volumes Publishing, 2006.

Tabernacle Baptist Church. "Spurgeon's Maxims for Living." Hanover Park, IL. http://www.spurgeon.us/quotes.htm.

"ThinkExist Quotation Database." Accessed August 16, 2011. http://www.thinkexist.com.

"Tom Peters Company Website." Accessed August 10, 2011. http://www.tompeters.com.

Tracy, Brian. *Eat That Frog!* San Francisco: Berrett-Khoehler Publishers, 2007.

Walton, Sam. *Sam Walton: Made in America*. New York: Bantam Books, 1993.

Wikipedia. "Focus." Accessed September 12, 2011. http://en.wikipedia.org/wiki/Focus.

Wikipedia. "Harald Bluetooth." Accessed August 29, 2011. http:// en.wikipedia.org/wiki/Harald_I_of_Denmark.

Wikipedia. "John Grisham." Accessed on August 19, 2011. http:// en.wikipedia.org/wiki/John_Grisham.

Wikipedia. "Károly Takács." Accessed on August 19, 2011. http:// www.en.wikipedia.org/wiki/K%C3%A1roly _Tak%C3%A1cs.

Wikipedia. "Steve Jobs." Accessed August 18, 2011. http:// en.wikipedia.org/wiki/Steve_Jobs.

Wilson, Michael and Rod Serling. *Planet of the Apes*. Directed by Franklin J. Shaffner. Twentieth Century Fox, Released April 3, 1968.

Wooden, John. *Wooden: A Lifetime of Observations and Reflections On and Off the Court*. New York: McGraw-Hill, 1997.

Woodward, Orrin. *RESOLVED: 13 Resolutions for LIFE*. Flint: Obstacles Press, 2011.

Yaeger, Don. "The Most Important Golf Story of the Year (That You Likely Never Heard About)." *Success Magazine*. September 2010.

YouTube. "Patrick Henry Hughes – Inspirational Story." Video submitted by kpmac1. Accessed August 3, 2011. http://www. youtube.com/watch?v=-qTiYA1WiY8.

Ziglar, Zig. "Goals." Cassette Tape, Produced by Nightingale-Conant Audio.

Ziglar, Zig. *Over the Top*. Nashville: Thomas Nelson Publishers, 1997.